Ras il-Wardija Sanctuary Revisited

A re-assessment of the evidence and newly-informed interpretations of a Punic-Roman sanctuary in Gozo (Malta)

George Azzopardi

ARCHAEOPRESS ARCHAEOLOGY

Archaeopress Publishing Ltd
13-14 Market Square
Bicester
Oxfordshire OX26 6AD
www.archaeopress.com

ISBN 978 1 78491 669 5
ISBN 978 1 78491 670 1 (e-Pdf)

© Archaeopress and George Azzopardi 2017

Cover image: Ras il-Wardija sanctuary seen from the air.
The sanctuary stands on the promontory seen in the foreground. (Photo: The author)

All rights reserved. No part of this book may be reproduced, in any form or
by any means, electronic, mechanical, photocopying or otherwise,
without the prior written permission of the copyright owners.

This book is available direct from Archaeopress or from our website www.archaeopress.com

To the memory
of
the late Paul Spiteri

Contents

List of Figures ii
Preface v

Chapter 1
1.1 Introducing the sanctuary site at Ras il-Wardija 1
1.2 History of research and existing literature 2
1.3 Objectives, aims, approach, and method of this study 2
1.4 Background to the Maltese islands: a brief historical profile 3

Chapter 2
2.1 Ras il-Wardija and its regional context: geographical extent and topography 6
2.2 Continuous human presence and occupation 6
2.3 Maritime connections and related activities 9
2.4 Seeking divine protection at sea 11

Chapter 3
3.1 The toponym 'Ras il-Wardija' 16
3.2 Origins and development of the sanctuary complex 16
3.3 Relationship between the sanctuary and the physical form of the landscape 18
3.4 Visual domination of the seascape 19
3.5 The temple building on the first terrace 23
3.6 The cave and ancillary features on the fifth terrace 27
3.7 Sacrality of doors: doorways with offering holes or other sacred features 40
3.8 Stone worship 43
3.9 Possible mysteries and the enigmatic cruciform and 'flying' figures 49
3.10 Regulating relations through ritual 60

Chapter 4
4.1 Closure of the site 61
4.2 Concluding observations 61

Appendix I 63
Appendix II 66
Bibliography 67
General Index 74

List of Figures

Figure 1. Map of the Maltese islands. It shows the location of Ras il-Wardija on the island of Gozo and other relevant sites on both islands 1

Figure 2. Table of Maltese chronology 4

Figure 3. Clay statuette head. The head (Max. Height: 8 cm) is alleged to have been found in a cistern at Tar-Rokon, in San Lawrenz, Gozo. It is now kept at the Gozo Museum of Archaeology 7

Figure 4. Stem of *oinochoe* (left) and a complete example (right). The stem (Max. Height: 7 cm) was found in the back-garden of a private residence in Triq il-Wileġ, San Lawrenz, Gozo. Now kept at the Gozo Museum of Archaeology 8

Figure 5. Aerial view of Ras il-Wardija sanctuary. The sanctuary is arrowed in the foreground while Xlendi is slightly visible to the right in the background. Photo taken in 1974 10

Figure 6. Another view of Ras il-Wardija sanctuary from the air. The sanctuary is arrowed in the foreground while Dwejra inlet is visible in the background 10

Figure 7. Lead anchor stock from Xlendi. The stock carries astragal representation on each of its arms testifying to mariners' fears and their superstitious beliefs. The set of astragals on the right is enlarged inset. The stock is on display at the Gozo Museum of Archaeology 11

Figure 8. A c. third to first-century BC Greek terracotta mask of Dionysos (left) and a convex ceramic object with relief globules on its outer surface (right). The latter (Max. Height: 19.5 cm) was retrieved from the seabed at the mouth of Xlendi Bay and is now on display at the Gozo Museum of Archaeology. Besides the beard in imitation of a grape cluster, the former (Height: 12.7 cm) carries also a tall crown of ivy leaves. Similar examples can be seen in the Pushkin State Museum of Fine Arts in Moscow. The lack of mouth and eye openings would seem to exclude use of the mask in drama performances and, thus, would confirm its votive or ritual character 12

Figure 9. Women engaged in ritual activity around a Dionysos mask mounted on a pole. The pole is also adorned with garments and other paraphernalia symbolic of Dionysos. Shown on an Athenian red-figure stamnos by the Villa Giulia Painter, *c.* 450 BC. Height: 47.4 cm; Diameter: 33.4 cm. Museum of Fine Arts, Boston. Gift of Edward Perry Warren. Accession No: 90. 155a 13

Figure 10. Standards mounted on poles on a ship depicted on a sacrificial stela from Carthage. The standards carry symbols of Tinnit / Tanit on prow and stern and a caduceus in the middle 14

Figure 11. Fatima's hand mounted on a pole on a modern Egyptian boat. This modern practice seems to carry forward the tradition of mounting standards with symbols on poles on sea vessels 14

Figure 12. Location map of Ras il-Wardija. The sanctuary's eight terraces are numbered I-VIII on the promontory 16

Figure 13. Ras il-Wardija promontory's sloping profile. The slope is viewed uphill from the first terrace towards the rock-cut cave on the fifth terrace. The temple remains on the first terrace can be seen in the foreground 17

Figure 14. Ras ir-Raħeb promontory (in Malta) from the air. To create a symbolic link between the land and the sea, a temple structure (arrowed) was purposely positioned on the prominent and conspicuous promontory 20

Figure 15. Ras il-Wardija dominating the seascape. The promontory's dominant position provides it with a view of the open sea for miles around 21

Figure 16. Ras il-Wardija viewed from Ras ir-Raħeb (in Malta) across the channel. The two sanctuaries on the respective promontories enjoyed a visual link 22

Figure 17. Plan of the temple remains. These are to be found on the first terrace of the sanctuary complex. Level readings are given in metres at various points on the plan 24

Figure 18. The so-called 'archaic temple' on Capo San Marco, Sardegna 25

Figure 19. The small Punic temple on the *isolotto di Su Cardolinu* at Chia (ancient Bithia), Sardegna 25

Figure 20. Plan of the rock-cut cave. The cave is to be found on the fifth terrace and has an internal U-shaped bench. Different levels are given in metres at various points on the plan 28

Figure 21. Niche 5 inside the rock-cut cave. A cruciform figure was centrally carved on the niche's internal wall. Two side-cuts that may have accommodated a shelf beneath the cruciform figure are also visible 29

Figure 22. Figure in 'flying' attitude. It was carved on wall A, between niches 1 and 2 inside the rock-cut cave 29

Figure 23. Small cruciform figure (arrowed) shown on top of a 'flying'(?) figure. It was carved on wall C, on the left side of niche 5 inside the rock-cut cave 29

Figure 24. General plan of the rock-cut cave in relation to the external features on the fifth terrace 30

Figure 25. Marks of stone extraction on the third terrace 31

Figure 26. The banqueting hall of the Dionysiac cowherds (*boukoloi*) at Pergamon, in Asia Minor (modern Turkey). The interior of this hall was divided into two facing banqueting rooms, each equipped with U-shaped benches or couches..32

Figure 27. The rock-cut benches / couches running parallel to the cave's facade. The U-shaped arrangement of the two facing spaces may have formed an extension (inside a roofed structure) to the U-shaped arrangement inside the cave. The arrangement also looks very similar to that in the banqueting hall at Pergamon shown in Figure 26..33

Figure 28. The cave interior with its U-shaped bench / couch arrangement and niches 33

Figure 29. A banqueting scene inside the cave. An artist's impression...34

Figure 30. An extension to the 'bench' and 'pavement' at the passage's point of intersection in front of the cave. This was done by inserting two perpendicular stones along two edges of a rock-cut offering table 36

Figure 31. Offering table and an intriguing sign (enlarged inset). The offering table was situated at the southernmost extent of the passage outside the cave. The intriguing sign was engraved very close to it and may have been associated with offerings 37

Figure 32. The sign at the Punic tophet of Sant' Antioco, in Sardegna. It is engraved on a high rock outcrop at the said tophet and is similar to the one from Ras il-Wardija shown in Figure 31 37

Figure 33. The rock-cut basin or pool on the fifth terrace 38

Figure 34. The rock-cut water cistern on the fifth terrace..38

Figure 35. Stone trough found in the rock-cut basin or pool. It was one of eleven small stone troughs retrieved from the muddy infill of the said basin or pool and which are now kept in storage at the Gozo Museum of Archaeology 39

Figure 36. Stone pyramidal 'cippus' or betyl. Assuming the shape of a pyramid, it stands on a base or pedestal as if to highlight the pyramid's significance. It is kept in storage at the Gozo Museum of Archaeology 43

Figure 37. Plan of the temple on the first terrace showing the findspot (encircled) of the pyramidal 'cippus' or betyl. The latter was found between the external wall of the temple and the presumed *temenos* wall, near the temple's entrance and the offering table in front of the said entrance.........................44

Figure 38. Pyramidal betyl claimed to represent Tanit. It was found in the small 'archaic temple' on Capo San Marco, Sardegna 45

Figure 39. Pyramidal betyl from the southern necropolis at Tharros, Sardegna. It is on display at the Archaeological Museum of Cabras, Sardegna..46

Figure 40. The pyramidal betyl as it might have looked inside the temple on the first terrace. An artist's impression with a cut-out view showing the interior. The betyl might have stood on a plinth, facing the temple's entrance and the offering table beyond from where it could have received offerings.....................47

Figure 41. A small stone 'column' betyl with a spiral rendering. It was found deposited above the offering table and within the basin created with the insertion of two stones around the same offering table at the passage intersection in front of the cave. It is now kept in storage at the Gozo Museum of Archaeology 48

Figure 42. The offering table at the bottom of the basin at the passage intersection in front of the cave. The basin was created with the insertion of two stones around the exposed edges of the offering table. The small stone column came from the infill within this basin and above the offering table 48

Figure 43. The standing 'column' betyl overlooking the offering table. An artist's impression showing the 'column' betyl in relation to the offering table with which it was found associated and, thus, from where it could have received offerings...49

Figure 44. Schematic cruciform figure in relief from Nora (modern Pula), Sardegna. It appears on a stela from Nora's Punic tophet..50

Figure 45. Schematic cruciform figure in relief from Sulcis (Sant' Antioco), Sardegna. It appears on a stela from Sulcis' Punic tophet 50

Figure 46. A cruciform herm of the god Hermes. This herm is to be found at the Museo Nazionale Romano Palazzo Massimo, Rome 50

Figure 47. A Dionysiac scene shown on a late antique ivory pyxis. The scene shows the newly-born Dionysos Zagreos on an initiation throne and with outstretched hands. He is in the process of being lured before he is slain. The pyxis is in the Museo Civico Archeologico in Bologna, Italy 54

Figure 48. A cruciform structure carried in a marriage procession of Dionysos in Athens. The procession scene is shown on an Attic chous in the Metropolitan Museum of Art in New York 55

Figure 49. An aged silenus approaching the child Dionysos with the cruciform structure (arrowed). This was the same cruciform structure carried in proces-sion in Athens. The scene of the aged silenus with the cruciform structure appears on the lid of a Roman sarcophagus of *c.* 190 AD in the Walters Art Museum, Baltimore, Maryland (USA)..55

Figure 50. Bacchus / Dionysos on a triple cruciform herm. He is shown in assimilation with Apollo and Axiokersos on one of the three cruciform sides of the herm that represents three sets of deities. The triple cruciform herm comes from Tor Marancia in Rome but is, now, in the Vatican Museum 56

Figure 51. A probable representation of the Cretan Dionysos on a Minoan gem from Kydonia. Described as 'lord of the wild beasts', the figure on the gem is shown with outstretched hands evidently resting on the respective heads of two flanking lions. The gem is at the Ashmolean Museum, Oxford 56

Figure 52. The cruciform figure in niche / shrine 5 inside the cave. What appears to be a rising pole above the cruciform figure's head may perhaps recall the poles on which Dionysos' masks used to be set up in the manner shown in Figure 9 57

Figure 53. The cruciform figure with offerings in niche / shrine 5 inside the cave. As it might have been itself an object of worship, the cruciform figure could have received offerings on a shelf inserted beneath as shown in this artist's impression 58

Figure 54. A Mediaeval graffito of a cruciform figure at the *Tour* of Domme (Dordogne, France). It was engraved on one of the walls of the towers flanking the gate of the *Tour* of Domme evidently by one of the Templar knights imprisoned there...59

Figure 55. The entire funerary monument set up to the memory of a young deceased girl by her mother. Discovered at 'Rabato, Notabile' in Malta around 1725, the (late) Roman funerary monument (including its inscription) was pictorially documented in its entirety by means of this sketch / preparatory drawing now preserved at the Hermitage in St Petersburg, Russia..64

Figure 56. The funerary monument set up to the memory of a young deceased girl by her mother in the lithograph published by Jean Hoüel. In this lithograph, the monument is seen flanked by another funerary monument and architectural specimens but, for some reason, its inscription is omitted 65

Preface

This book evolved from one of five major case studies presented by the author in his PhD thesis entitled 'Religious Landscapes and Identities of the Maltese islands in a Mediterranean Context: 700 BC-AD 500'. The thesis was presented to the Department of Archaeology at Durham University (UK) for the award of a doctorate in July 2014.

The case study in question dealt with a sanctuary site at Ras il-Wardija on the small Mediterranean island of Gozo and the present book constitutes an amplification and further development of that particular case study following a re-assessment of the existing data, especially data which has been largely overlooked or superficially treated and interpreted in related literature. In addition to this re-assessment, newly-discovered data (particularly concerning the region) and parallels from comparable sites and ritual activities contribute towards fresh observations and interpretations.

In general, the book may also contribute to fill a major *lacuna* with respect to the sanctuary site at Ras il-Wardija. So far, this site does not seem to have been given the attention it rightly deserves as a site which is also unique in its own right. To make good for this 'deficiency', this study seeks to highlight the sanctuary at Ras il-Wardija as another significant site on the religious map of the ancient Mediterranean and, as such, a site with which confrontations or comparisons can also be made.

At the same time, and perhaps more importantly, this volume also seeks to enhance the knowledge available to date about religious practices, experiences, and expressions in the ancient Mediterranean world. But it could also show how these may have possibly migrated with the movements of peoples across the Mediterranean basin, thus also lending its contribution to the field of comparative studies.

Chapter 1

1.1 Introducing the sanctuary site at Ras il-Wardija

The coastal stretch on the western side of the central Mediterranean island of Gozo, near Malta, is marked by a pronounced headland facing south-west and known as 'Ras il-Wardija'. Best accessed from Ta' Kerċem village or from the nearby one of Santa Luċija (Figure 1), this coastal headland is host to a sanctuary site spread on eight terraces going uphill from the first terrace situated by the cliff edge rising about 120 m above sea level (*MISSIONE 1964*: 167). The terrace formation appears to have been a later intervention, probably for agricultural purposes (see 3.2 below). However, here and henceforth, the sanctuary areas, features, or finds shall be related to these terraces for ease of reference.

As will be seen in 3.5-6 below, the surviving and most important structural remains of this sanctuary consist of what appears to have been a temple and an artificial quadrangular cave on the first and fifth terraces respectively. The cave has rock-cut features both inside and outside in front of it. The floor features inside and immediately outside the cave are, now, buried. The presumed temple built on the first terrace seems to have been a centre of ritual activity that appears to have extended to the fifth terrace (see 3.5, 3.9 below) where a cave was dug and a room might have been later built in extension to it to provide the set-up for ritual gatherings and ceremonies. Other associated features on the fifth terrace are a water cistern (with a rectangular opening) and a large quadrangular open basin (or pool) both of which

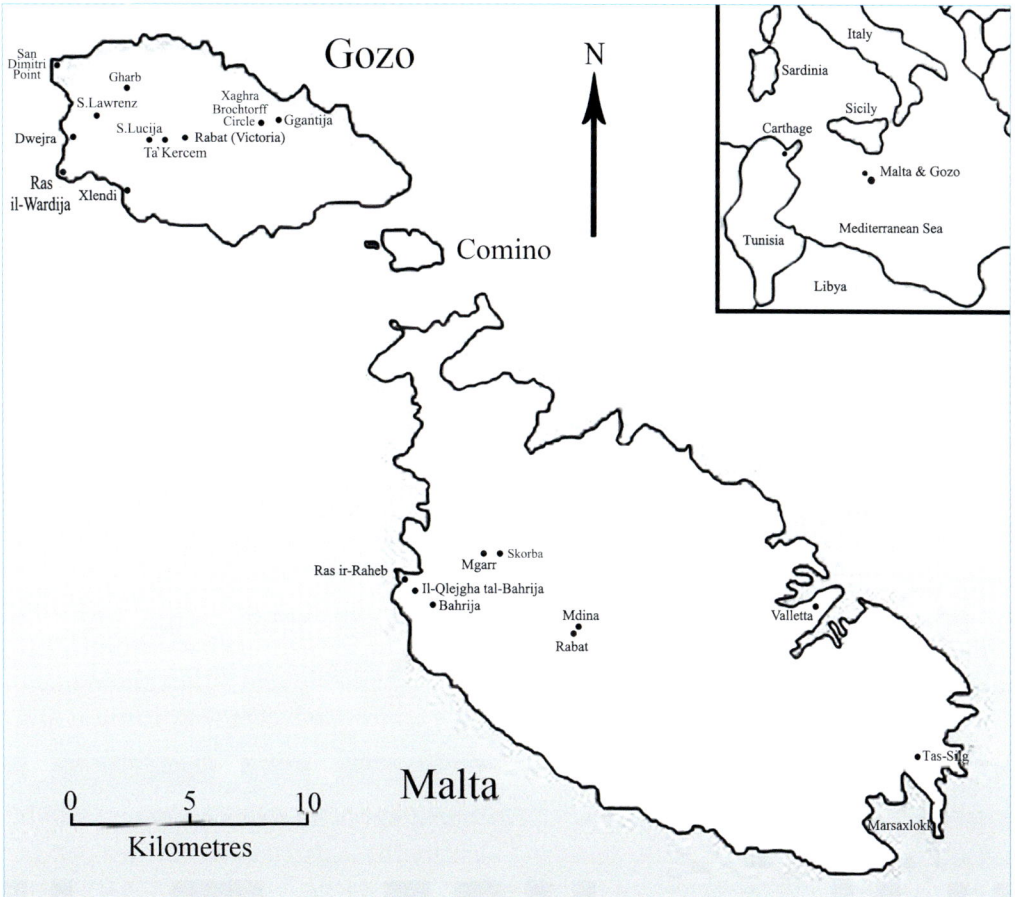

Figure 1. Map of the Maltese islands. It shows the location of Ras il-Wardija on the island of Gozo and other relevant sites on both islands. (After www.geocities.ws/maltashells/NatHist.html).

are also cut in the rock surface. These may have been ancillary facilities with a role to play in the above-mentioned ceremonies while the remaining terraces could have provided the setting where processions or drama performances of a religious character were enacted.

On the basis of the unearthed pottery, the sanctuary appears to have been in use from around the 3rd century BC (late Punic period in the Maltese islands) to the 2nd century AD, and, possibly, even as late as the 4th century AD (late Roman period) (see 3.2 below).

1.2 History of research and existing literature

The sanctuary site was shortlisted for eventual excavation following a reconnaissance exercise involving a number of sites in the Maltese islands that looked promising in terms of their archaeological potential (*MISSIONE 1964*: 167-8). This exercise was undertaken in 1962 under the direction of Michelangelo Cagiano de Azevedo of the Catholic University of Milan and as part of a research initiative – including archaeological excavations – entrusted to the *Missione Archeologica Italiana a Malta* and which the latter was to develop over the following years.

The site was, in fact, excavated between 1964 and 1967 by the above-mentioned *Missione Archeologica Italiana a Malta* of the Institute of Near Eastern Studies of the University of Rome (*MISSIONE 1964-7*). The excavation method focused more on buried structures and features as the site's stratigraphy was found to have been disturbed perhaps as a result of agricultural activity in later times. But although found disturbed, the ceramic repertoire was found to be homogeneous and, thus, did not appear to have been extraneous to the site. Thus, it could provide a reliable basis at least for a broad dating of the site.

The results attained from the excavation were published in a series of four preliminary reports by the said institution but, apart from these reports, no major publications on this site are known to have ever made their appearance. The Ras il-Wardija sanctuary does, at times, feature alongside other sites of a similar nature or of the same period in books or journal papers but, even in such instances, the material concerning the sanctuary of Ras il-Wardija as laid out in these publications is generally a synthesis or a re-elaboration of the data given in the *Missione*'s preliminary reports without any serious attempt to provide an analysis or any interpretations other than those already supplied by the Italian archaeologists of the *Missione* in the 1960s.

1.3 Objectives, aims, approach, and method of this study

Whilst bringing out its uniqueness, this study seeks to look at the sanctuary site of Ras il-Wardija first within its own regional context and then also within the wider religious and cultural context of the Mediterranean. To this end, due emphasis is afforded to the landscape aspect and, in particular, to the religious landscape. Parallels are drawn between this site and sites of a similar nature across the Mediterranean not only in terms of physical landscape but also (wherever possible) in terms of certain ritual practices and experiences which certain Mediterranean religious sites and the sanctuary site at Ras il-Wardija in Gozo seem to have shared on the basis of similar features or characteristics they exhibit. The aim of this adopted approach is to demonstrate that, ultimately and although unique in its own right, the sanctuary at Ras il-Wardija formed part of the wider Mediterranean cultural and religious scenario.

Prior to a detailed study of the sanctuary itself, an examination of its regional context will help locate nearby and any possibly associated settlements and identify the activities that formed part of the daily life in these settlements. But, as suggested mainly by its coastal location, the sanctuary seems to have been essentially connected to maritime life. The neighbouring coastline with its cliffs, inlet, and harbour, thus, features prominently as part of the sanctuary's regional set-up. Therefore, this study will also look into the life of the maritime people who, through their visits to the nearby inlet and harbour – and, presumably, to the sanctuary too – are expected to have contributed to the sanctuary's dynamism and significance in no small measure.

Wherever possible, data are drawn from primary sources, particularly the Museums Annual Reports which give yearly accounts and details of archaeological fieldwork and chance discoveries. But in many instances, features or finds have never been officially recorded or published. Nonetheless, as they often physically survive (and, thus, are subject to observation), they are included as well.

Then, this study moves on to focus on the sanctuary itself and its landscape but also affords due consideration to artefacts it yielded in an attempt to reconstruct ritual practices and experiences at the sanctuary in its heyday and, possibly, identify any associated cults. Site data for this part of the study are also drawn from primary sources, relying heavily and almost exclusively on the reports of the excavations undertaken at Ras il-Wardija in the 1960s by the *Missione Archeologica Italiana a Malta* (*MISSIONE 1964-7*).

But the site is not looked at in isolation. To attain a more holistic picture in terms of both site itself and its related activities, this study also pays due attention not only to the regional but also to the wider Mediterranean context. The gathered data is, thus, synthesised and analysed with reference to wider literature not only to come up with interpretations regarding the site and its associated ritual practices but also to put the sanctuary within the contemporary religious context of the wider Mediterranean region.

1.4 Background to the Maltese islands: a brief historical profile

In various respects, the Maltese islands – comprising Malta (the largest of the group), Gozo, and Comino (the smallest and least inhabited island) – are akin to other Mediterranean islands particularly those that, like them, are to be found in the central part of the sea like Pantelleria, Sicily, and the Lipari islands, though not without their distinct characteristics. The physical landscape of the Maltese islands was shaped by geomorphological processes over thousands of years, resulting in a coastline marked by cliffs, promontories, open beaches and sheltered coves and a hinterland marked by hills, fertile plains, winding valleys, and settled areas. These topographical features also played their part to varying degrees in the unfolding developments that shaped Maltese history (and prehistory) within its broader Mediterranean context.

Situated at the very heart of the Mediterranean, the Maltese group of islands lay at the centre of a network of movements and activities which shaped the Mediterranean region – and not least the Maltese islands themselves – for many centuries. As a result, during the 7000 years or so of their occupation, the Maltese islands came in contact with various cultures: different prehistoric peoples (Neolithic, Temple Period, and Bronze Age), Phoenicians, Carthaginians, Romans, Byzantines, Sicilian-Arabs, Normans, Angevins, Aragonese, Knights Hospitallers of St John, and British (Figure 2). All of these were constantly competing for geographically strategic positions, for military exploitation, for influences, for political control, and for commercial markets in the Mediterranean (Fiorini and Mallia-Milanes 1991).

The Maltese islands appear to have been first settled around 5000 BC (Trump (with Cilia) 2004: 10, 23, 26, 54-5) and remained occupied ever since, though not uninterruptedly. But this study will focus on the early historical period of the islands starting around 700 BC. By this time, mainly through their commercial networks in the Mediterranean, the Phoenicians came in contact with the islanders. Initially, there may have been sporadic contacts that, gradually, consolidated themselves into a form of permanent presence. While the Phoenicians integrated themselves with the rest of the population, they introduced and adapted new ideas too as evidenced by their surviving material legacy (examples in Bonanno (with Cilia) 2005: 20-71). This period appears to have also ushered in a new settlement pattern with emphasis laid more on centrally-located urbanisation as exemplified by Melite (today's Rabat and Mdina) in Malta and Gaulos (today's Victoria) in Gozo. In the religious sphere, new cults were introduced (as can be shown,

Period	Phase	Duration
Early Neolithic	Għar Dalam	c. 5000 – 4300 BC
"	Grey Skorba	c. 4500 – 4400 BC
"	Red Skorba	c. 4400 – 4100 BC
Late Neolithic / Temple	Żebbuġ	c. 4100 – 3700 BC
"	Mġarr	c. 3800 – 3600 BC
"	Ġgantija	c. 3600 – 3200 BC
"	Saflieni	c. 3300 – 3000 BC
"	Tarxien	c. 3150 – 2500 BC
Bronze Age	Tarxien Cemetery	c. 2500 – 1500 BC
"	Borġ in-Nadur	c. 1500 – 700 BC
"	Baħrija	c. 900 – 700 BC
Phoenician		c. 700 – 550 BC
Punic		c. 550 – 218 BC
Roman	Republican	c. 218 – 27 BC
"	Imperial	27 BC – AD 535
Medieval	Byzantine	AD 535 – 870
"	Muslim	AD 870 – 1091
"	Norman	AD 1091 – 1194
"	Hohenstaufen	AD 1194 – 1266
"	Angevin	AD 1266 – 1283
"	Aragonese	AD 1283 – 1530
Early Modern	Knights	AD 1530 – 1798
"	French	AD 1798 – 1800
Modern	British	AD 1800 – 1964

Figure 2. Table of Maltese chronology.

for instance, at Tas-Silġ sanctuary) although, initially, these may have been syncretised cults developed from earlier ones.

By the time the Phoenicians were well established in the western Mediterranean, the city of Carthage (itself under Phoenician domination) assumed a leading role in the western Mediterranean, comprising also the Maltese islands as from the late 6th or early 5th century BC. From now on, the Maltese islands found themselves also immersed in the political and military intricacies that, by then, were characterising the central Mediterranean as Carthage and the newly-emerging power – Rome – were competing for power and supremacy.

This situation gradually ended with the balance tipping in favour of Rome and the Maltese islands shifted to Roman control around 218 BC. (Bonanno (with Cilia) 2005: 35, 131). This ushered in a long period of around seven centuries during which the Maltese islands were to participate – to greater or lesser degrees – in the unfolding developments that shaped the Roman world. In the initial stages of Roman occupation, 'Maltese' culture and religion were a blend of reworked Phoenician / Punic, Greek, and Roman elements as evidenced, for instance, by contemporary coinage but, in peripheral areas of the islands, these hybrid culture and religion are likely to have survived longer.

The Roman control of the islands lasted when, around AD 445, the islands may have been taken over by the Vandals and, then, possibly by the Ostrogoths around AD 477 until, finally, they were incorporated within the Byzantine empire in AD 535. But from the 1st century AD onwards and in circumstances which, to date, remain largely obscure, Christianity had already started to develop alongside other cults until, gradually, it took over in a rather syncretised form. The material record for early Christianity or for any other cults (alongside Christianity) in late antiquity is negligible; possibly, having been destroyed.

As shown above, in the sphere of colonial domination, the Maltese and Gozitans changed masters more than once when their occupation shifted amongst different competing powers. These shifts brought about changes in colonial relationships and also in alliances not only in the internal realm of politics but also in that of religion, further confirming the close relationship and mutual influence between these two realms.

Furthermore, during all periods of domination by external powers, the Maltese at large were imbued with a feeling of subordination and dependence very typical of colonised communities. Yet, somehow sidelined from the mainstream of the dominating (and urban) culture, the rural communities managed to maintain, to a greater extent and for quite long periods of time, a re-worked but autonomous culture. On the other hand and largely with respect to the remaining categories of Maltese society, external domination enabled contacts bringing in influences and ideas from outside not least in the religious sphere. Along with the somewhat 'conservative' character typical of rural cultures, this contact with changing and diverse external cultures over such a long span of time has helped fashion the Maltese cultural identity into a multi-cultural one (Fiorini and Mallia-Milanes 1991).

Chapter 2

2.1 Ras il-Wardija and its regional context: geographical extent and topography

As stated earlier, Ras il-Wardija is a high coastal promontory facing south-west. It is flanked by Xlendi harbour to the south and Dwejra inlet, an anchorage or sheltering port, to the west. These are the only places providing access to and from the sea as the remaining coast along the Ras il-Wardija area consists of sheer cliffs.

The general topography of the area is rather varied with plateaus, hills, and winding valleys opening up into Dwejra and Xlendi bays. The Xlendi valley remains green practically all year round as it is fed by perennial springs in the Tal-Lunzjata valley which is a tributary of the larger Xlendi valley, the Għajn Tuta spring, and by other perennial springs likewise feeding an old public wash-house in the small village of Fontana (Għajn il-Kbira), not far from the larger village of Ta' Kerċem.

The present-day villages in the area of Ras il-Wardija stand on plateaus surrounded by the hills and quite close to the valleys. These villages include Għarb, San Lawrenz, Ta' Kerċem, and the hamlet of Santa Luċija. On the basis of archaeological evidence examined further below, their origins are known to date back at least to Classical times. Though now no longer inhabited, some of the hills – like Għajn Abdul and, possibly, even Ta' Dbieġi – also provide evidence of human occupation in earlier times. Għajn Abdul, for instance, hosted cave dwellings since Neolithic times.

The valleys, in particular, are home to terraced fields with good agricultural soil. Fertile fields are located on the bottoms of Tal-Lunzjata and Xlendi valleys and terraced ones flank the sides of these same valleys. More fertile fields are to be found on the slopes of hills like Għajn Abdul and the adjacent Għar Ilma and in their respective surrounding areas. Both of these hills have perennial springs from which they derive their respective names: Għajn Abdul ('the spring of Abdul') and Għar Ilma ('the cave of water' or 'the cave from where water springs forth'). Other terraced fields are to be found on the sides of the Dwejra valley and of its tributary Wied Pisklu (Pisklu valley) and on the slopes of Ta' Dbieġi hill. This extensively agricultural region bears witness to the extent to which the population of the area relied – until relatively recent times – on agriculture for its subsistence.

The region is also relatively rich in one of the most commonly-sought mineral resources, namely good building stone. To this day, the island of Gozo is supplied with Globigerina limestone from quarries in the area. Although most of the quarries operating today are modern, evidence of stone extraction from this region in earlier times is attested too, particularly from Ras il-Wardija itself as will be shown further below.

2.2 Continuous human presence and occupation

The south-west region of Gozo seems to have attracted human settlement since prehistoric times. Caves at Għajn Abdul provide evidence of human presence there as early as *c.* 5000 BC in the Għar Dalam phase of the Neolithic (*MAR* 1969: 5). The earliest people inhabiting the caves at Għajn Abdul are likely to have arrived via Xlendi Bay or, perhaps, the bay of Dwejra, after a sea journey from nearby Sicily.

Later in the prehistoric period – possibly, during the Temple period / Late Neolithic – another settlement may have sprung up near the later village of Ta' Kerċem. The remains of a megalithic structure were brought to light in this village early in the 20th century (*MAR* 1905-6: 3). A prehistoric burial of the Tarxien phase (3150-2500 BC) – the only prehistoric burial ever discovered in the south-west region – came to light in 2008 in the area where presumably the above-mentioned megalithic remains had been earlier found (personal observation). Although excavated, this burial is still awaiting publication.

Human presence at Ta' Kerċem seems to have remained continuous in succeeding periods. In the beginning of the 20th century, remains of a house described as 'Phoenician' were found not very far from the prehistoric megalithic structure mentioned above but were destroyed soon after discovery (*MAR* 1907: 3). The small Late Roman catacomb of Għar Gerduf on the outskirts of the same village indicates activity at the end of the early historic period too.

Human presence and activity in and around the caves at nearby Għajn Abdul likewise remained more or less continuous throughout later prehistoric phases and even as late as the Mediaeval and Modern periods (*MAR* 1969: 5-6). The nearby fresh water spring and fertile soils might explain this likewise continuous human presence and activity at Għajn Abdul.

Human occupation and activity is also evidenced at the village of San Lawrenz and at the adjacent one of Għarb at least from Classical times onwards. However, most of the evidence comes from accidental and unrecorded discoveries but, in several cases, the finds themselves at least managed to make their way to the archaeology museum of the island where they are still preserved. Of notable significance are the sites of Tar-Rokon at San Lawrenz and Ix-Xaqqufija (or Ta' Xaqqufiet) at Għarb. Tar-Rokon yielded a statuette head of the late 6th or early 5th century BC allegedly found in a cistern (Figure 3) as well as a number of burials never officially reported and documented. These burials are alleged to have yielded a number of clay cinerary urns of the Classical period which were later donated by their private owners to the Cathedral museum in the Gozo Citadel (Tony Mercieca and Joseph Bezzina personal communication). Ix-Xaqqufija (or Ta' Xaqqufiet) is the site of huge foundation stones reported by the eighteenth-century Gozitan scholar and antiquarian Giovanni Pietro Francesco Agius de Soldanis to have been discovered there in 1743 along with a large rectangular water cistern next to them (NLM, Libr. MS 145: f. 54). On the basis of the evident association between the structure (to which the huge foundation stones belonged) and the nearby water cistern and also on the basis of the respective descriptions he provides, Ix-Xaqqufija (or Ta' Xaqqufiet) could have been the site of an agricultural estate or a farm complex perhaps datable to Roman times (Azzopardi 2012: 58). From the same place, the same scholar recorded the discovery, in 1748, of a large marble statue of Julia Domna (wife of Lucius Septimius Severus, Roman emperor from AD 193 to 211) whose head he kept in his own collection (Agius de Soldanis 1750: 26). As agricultural estates or farm complexes were owned by wealthy individuals who not only often had a residence attached to the same estate or farm complex but could also afford to have them adorned with statues, a possible association between this statue and the presumed agricultural estate or farm complex cannot be completely ruled out (Azzopardi 2012: 58-9). Whether agricultural or otherwise, anthropogenic activity there seems to be also suggested by the surface scatter of ceramic fragments implied by the toponym itself – Ix-Xaqqufija / Ta' Xaqqufiet: 'the field littered with ceramic fragments' (Azzopardi 2012: 59).

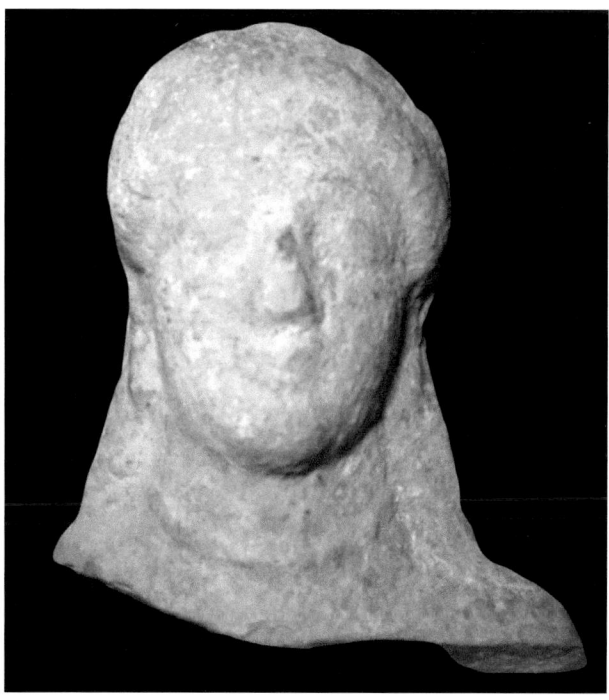

Figure 3. Clay statuette head. The head (Max. Height: 8 cm) is alleged to have been found in a cistern at Tar-Rokon, in San Lawrenz, Gozo. It is now kept at the Gozo Museum of Archaeology. (Photo: The author).

Apart from agriculture, the local people also engaged themselves in the processing of certain agricultural products. Not only fields are abundantly present in the area surrounding the two adjacent villages of San Lawrenz and Għarb but a rock-cut wine-press on the surface of one of the sides of Wied Pisklu in the limits of San Lawrenz (Jaccarini and Cauchi 1999: 427-8, 433, Plate 8) might indicate grape-pressing (even if, perhaps, not on a large scale) and, indirectly, viticulture in the nearby fields.

Viticulture and wine production would logically imply also wine consumption. The lowermost part of the stem and base of an elegantly decorated *oinochoe* (wine jug) of the 3rd century BC (Figure 4, left) was found in the back-garden of a private residence in Triq il-Wileġ, San Lawrenz in soil claimed to have had earlier originated from the site of the village parish church when this was being enlarged in the 1950s (Anne Monsarrat personal communication). It is currently on permanent display at the Gozo Archaeology Museum. The surviving lowermost part of the *oinochoe*'s stem is decorated in a sea-wave pattern which like the rest of the surviving band decoration is painted with red ochre (Nicola Attard Montalto personal communication). On the basis of precisely similar vessels, this *oinochoe* is extremely likely to have had its shoulder part decorated with ivy leaves (Figure 4, right). The ivy was a symbol – and, sometimes, representation – of the wine god Dionysos (Kerényi 1976: 196 (including footnotes 22, 24), 289, 372, Plates 89, 130C). The occurrence of this kind of decoration would seem to put the wine container (i.e. the *oinochoe*) in close association with the wine god (i.e. Dionysos). The preference or choice of this kind of container (even if it was imported) with this kind of decoration could further suggest that Dionysos may have already enjoyed familiarity or, perhaps, even worship in Gozo by that time. In correspondence with this interpretation, can one think of the possibility that the sea-wave decoration on the lowermost part of the *oinochoe*'s stem may have represented the sea-borne spread of viticulture / wine and of Dionysos' cult along with trade, which could be also the same manner in which viticulture / wine and Dionysos' worship may have reached Malta and Gozo? (see 2.4 below).

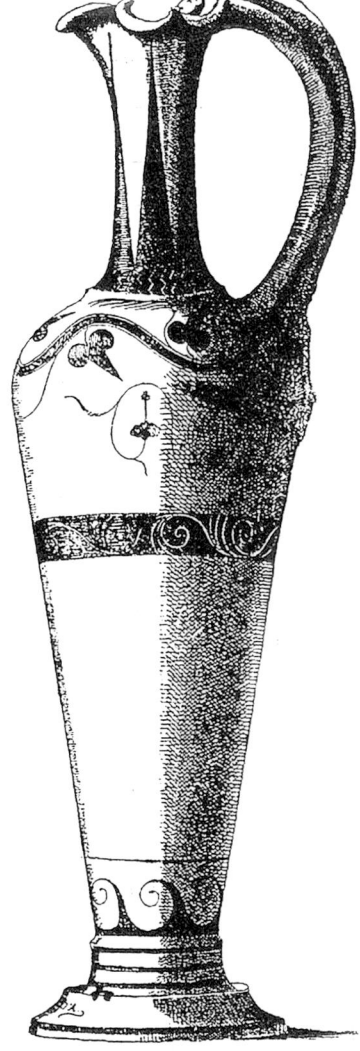

So far, the only evidence for ancient stone quarrying comes from Ras il-Wardija itself (see below). However, given the wide availability of good building stone in the whole area, it seems likely that people in this area engaged themselves in this useful activity in ancient times too. This may lead us to plausibly suggest that, along with agriculture and some degree of maritime activity like fishing, stone extraction might have been another main human occupation in the area.

The extent of human presence in the Ras il-Wardija area may be further testified by a substantial number

Figure 4. Stem of *oinochoe* (left) and a complete example (right). The stem (Max. Height: 7 cm) was found in the back-garden of a private residence in Triq il-Wileġ, San Lawrenz, Gozo. Now kept at the Gozo Museum of Archaeology. (Left photo: The author; Source of example on the right: Delattre 1906: 41(Fig. 5)).

of both natural and man-made small 'rock-shelters' noticeable in the entire area (particularly in the countryside) if, as suggested by the type of rock-cut recesses and troughs found therein, these were used as burials possibly in late Classical antiquity. The people in the area may have been involved in the upkeep (and, possibly, also in the erection) of the sanctuary at Ras il-Wardija. In any event, the sanctuary's probable use by visitors to Xlendi and Dwejra bays is expected to have brought the local community into contact with external people and their cultures.

2.3 Maritime connections and related activities

Maritime activity associated with the south-west region of Gozo is also quite strongly evidenced particularly in the bays of Xlendi and Dwejra. This maritime activity may have complemented other human activity in the hinterland and the coastal sanctuary at Ras il-Wardija may have served as a catalyst of this complementarity.

In Classical antiquity, Xlendi harbour might have also been inhabited as seems to be indicated by a single but collective Classical period tomb discovered there (*MAR* 1923-4: III; 1965: 3-4). But above all, the harbour appears to have witnessed a relatively intensive maritime activity over a long stretch of time. Visiting cargo vessels to the port (or leaving the port) are attested by a number of wrecks located at or not far from the mouth of the bay and spanning broadly from the late 7th century BC to the 5th or 7th century AD on the basis of ceramic material (largely amphorae) from the seabed (Atauz 2004: 23-4, 28-32, 64 (Fig. 18)-6, 375-81; Azzopardi 2013: 288-90; Gambin 2005: 17-8; *MAR* 1961: 6-7, Fig. 5; *Report 1961 & 1970*; Trump and Mallia 1964).

Very significantly, Xlendi is situated along the sea-route that would have been taken by any vessels crossing between North Africa and the eastern coast of Sicily. Furthermore, the harbour itself must have been more spacious as it extended inland by some 200 m more than it does nowadays (Gambin 2003: 134 (Fig. 1), 143; 2005: 16, 18-9). Coupled with the relatively small dimensions of ancient sea-vessels, this may have enabled the ancient harbour to accommodate many vessels, their crews, and the activities which these would have generated.

Further west, there is Dwejra Bay. Being smaller than Xlendi, it might have not offered the same facilities but its deep and sheltered inlet behind Fungus Rock might have served as a suitable anchorage, perhaps providing temporary shelter and some basic services to visiting vessels (Gambin 2005: 17, 20). Undated cart-ruts in the Dwejra Bay area bear witness to some degree of human activity there, perhaps in association with the port itself.

The seabed extending from San Dimitri Point (further north of Dwejra Bay) down to Dwejra, Ras il-Wardija, Xlendi, and even further beyond to the south seems to be littered with material debris associated with sea-borne activity (local fishermen personal communication). The above-mentioned Xlendi wrecks lie within this stretch. Three lead anchor stocks and one lead anchor collar from Xlendi Bay and another lead anchor stock found in isolation on the seabed off Ras il-Wardija promontory (where the sanctuary is situated) (Azzopardi, Gambin and Zerafa 2013: 23, 25-6(Fig. 3c), 27(Fig. 4h)-30) may have come from any of the ships wrecked at Xlendi Bay or from any others possibly wrecked in that area.

The presence of sanctuaries (including later Christian ones) could aid and guide seafarers in their navigation and could also serve as places of devotion for the same people (see 3.4 below). For these reasons, these sanctuaries were located not only in dominant positions (where they could be seen from afar) on promontories, on islands, or in association with harbours but also in places rich in cultic significance (Aulisa 2014: 130-1; also as in 134-5, 138-9; Galdi 2014: 151-2, 164).

Enjoying good views over the sea-route approaching Xlendi on one side (Figure 5) and over Dwejra itself on the other side (Figure 6), the Ras il-Wardija headland accommodates the sanctuary which is seen not only from Dwejra but also from any vessel far out at sea on its way to either Dwejra or Xlendi or plying the North Africa-Sicily route.

Coupled with the visibility the sanctuary enjoyed, the known shipwrecks may explain the significance of the sanctuary and of its location. The wrecks concentrated at the mouth of Xlendi Bay would seem to indicate that approaching Xlendi harbour might have not been an easy task under certain wind conditions. Caught in such conditions aided by underwater currents generated by the reef at the mouth of the harbour, an approaching sea-vessel would have found it extremely difficult to make it to port safely. Ill-fate might have struck those infrequent vessels and their crews who, unaware of these perils, might have sometimes found themselves trapped in such a situation. On the other hand, for the more frequently visiting vessels and their crews, more familiar with the Gozitan coast, the Dwejra port might have provided a temporary shelter until the dangerous winds calmed down (Atauz 2004: 23, 28-9, 32, 66; Gambin 2005: 17).

Figure 5. Aerial view of Ras il-Wardija sanctuary. The sanctuary is arrowed in the foreground while Xlendi is slightly visible to the right in the background. Photo taken in 1974. (Photograph © NAG-National Archives Gozo).

Figure 6. Another view of Ras il-Wardija sanctuary from the air. The sanctuary is arrowed in the foreground while Dwejra inlet is visible in the background. (Photo: The author).

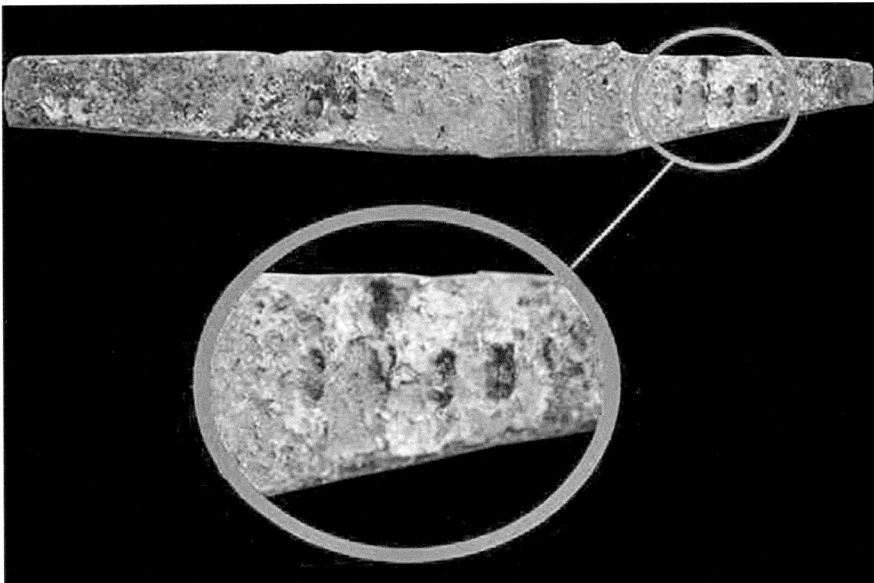

Figure 7. Lead anchor stock from Xlendi. The stock carries astragal representation on each of its arms testifying to mariners' fears and their superstitious beliefs. The set of astragals on the right is enlarged inset. The stock is on display at the Gozo Museum of Archaeology. (Photo: The author).

The fear sailors often experienced on account of these or similar perils is attested by one of the three lead anchor stocks retrieved from the mouth of Xlendi Bay (Figure 7). This particular stock carries, in representation, a set of four astragals (or sheep's knucklebones) mirrored on each of its arms (Gambin 2005: 18(Fig. 6); *MAR* 1961: 7, wherein the astragals are mistakenly identified as undecipherable letters). On account of their association with lot casting and the reading of omens, the astragals were believed to bring good luck and, thus, used to be sometimes reproduced (in a favourable combination) on the arms of anchor stocks in the belief that such anchors would bring good luck to the sailors at sea (Brody 1998: 84, 102; Radic-Rossi 2005: 34-5). This particular anchor from Xlendi, however, does not appear to have satisfied this expectation; unless it was simply abandoned, perhaps on getting irretrievably stuck.

Geographically located on the coast and, thus and very often, not far from harbours, maritime sanctuaries comprised veritable and suitable sacral points between land and sea (Aulisa 2014: 140). There could have been several factors – be they related to political, social, or economic considerations or to the site's interfacing location between land and sea – which led to the choice of the site for the location of a sanctuary. But the perils outlined above and sometimes encountered by vessels approaching Xlendi harbour might have generated the need of divine protection which could be sought from a place well visible when need arose or, else, whenever approaching or leaving harbour. The selected location, therefore, might have been intended to put the sanctuary within sight of incoming visitors from overseas who might have also visited it in thanksgiving soon after their safe arrival and / or before their departure to invoke a safe voyage (Gambin 2005: 16-7).

2.4 Seeking divine protection at sea

As vehicles for multidirectional mobility of people, goods, and ideas (Demetriou 2012: 23), maritime trade networks in which the Maltese islands were immersed opened up for them a world of religious ideologies, a wider pantheon of deities, and a diversity of ritual practices (Azzopardi 2014: 292).

A hollow convex ceramic object tapering at one end and with relief globules on its outer surface looking like a bunch of grapes (Figure 8, right) was retrieved from Xlendi Bay by a sport diver in the summer of 2005. It was found on the seabed at an approximate depth of 18 m and in close proximity to the western side of an isolated submerged rock or reef that is almost centrally located at the mouth of the bay. Following its retrieval, the find was deposited for permanent display at the Gozo Archaeology Museum by its finder in September of the same year (Steve Attard personal communication). The object does not

Figure 8. A c. third to first-century BC Greek terracotta mask of Dionysos (left) and a convex ceramic object with relief globules on its outer surface (right). The latter (Max. Height: 19.5 cm) was retrieved from the seabed at the mouth of Xlendi Bay and is now on display at the Gozo Museum of Archaeology. Besides the beard in imitation of a grape cluster, the former (Height: 12.7 cm) carries also a tall crown of ivy leaves. Similar examples can be seen in the Pushkin State Museum of Fine Arts in Moscow. The lack of mouth and eye openings would seem to exclude use of the mask in drama performances and, thus, would confirm its votive or ritual character. (Left photo credit: EdgarLOwen.com.; Right photo: The author).

exhibit any signs of breakage except along its widest end. It may have originated from a shipwreck unless it was accidentally dropped or deliberately thrown overboard perhaps in an act of ritual 'deposition'.

As the relief globules look much like a bunch of grapes, these may suggest that this object could have been part of a Dionysos Botrys face mask with a beard in imitation of a bunch of grapes (Figure 8, left). If so, it may date to the last centuries BC or to the early centuries AD. Signifying a bunch of grapes, 'Botrys' was sometimes used as a qualification of the wine-god Dionysos, while sometimes it designated a deity of grapes linked to the cycle of Dionysos (*LIMC* III/1: 143-4; III/2: 123(2-3)). In case this object was part of such a mask, was this mask on its way to be deposited by its owner – a mariner or a wine-merchant – perhaps as a votive offering at the nearby sanctuary of Ras il-Wardija?

For a long time, the mask had been a symbol of Dionysos and seems to have had a role to play in Dionysiac / Bacchic mysteries and celebrations (Nilsson 1985: 44, 97-8. See also Bowden 2010: 135; Henrichs 1993: 36-9; Kerényi 1976: 123, 192, 282-3, 286, 289, Plate 89; Nielsen 2014: 210(footnote 99)). In his *Georgics* (2. 388-9), Virgil recorded how effigies of Dionysos in the form of masks used to be suspended like *oscilla* from trees as part of Dionysiac rituals (see also Taylor 2005: 84-5). He also affirmed that, hung from trees, they also performed an apotropaic function as they were believed to guarantee an abundant agricultural yield (2. 390-2. See also Zampi 2002: 29(footnote 2)). But as Dionysiac imagery could be suspended from or attached to structural elements too (Taylor 2005: 93), particularly in shrines where they could be offered as the *oscilla* were (Macrobius, *Saturnalia* 1. 11. 48 cited in Taylor 2005: 101), it is thus possible that, unless it was hung on a ship as an apotropaic device providing protection to the (wine) cargo and to the ship and its crew (see also below), our presumed Dionysos' mask might have been destined to be hung in a similar manner perhaps as a votive offering at the sanctuary of Ras il-Wardija. Further below (see 3.6, 3.9) will be shown that Dionysos, in fact, might have been one of the deities in honour of whom rituals (possibly, involving also Dionysiac / Bacchic mysteries) could have been performed in this sanctuary.

But besides votive purposes, masks (like those of Dionysos) could have also served more specifically ritual purposes as also shown above. In Dionysiac festivities, for example, a participant could put on a mask of Dionysos in an act of self-identification with the god (Kerényi 1976: 314; see also 317, 353-5; Nielsen 2014: 213(Fig. 135)). But in certain ritual contexts, particularly those in connection with outdoor cults, such masks set up on poles or columns adorned with appropriate garments in a *tropaion* / trophy-like manner (Figure 9) might be used as temporary representations or manifestations of the deity to whom ritual offerings were made (Bianchi 1976: 35(81), Plate 81; Bowden 2010: 135; Brody 1998: 50; Gaifman 2012: 36(including Fig. 1.2), 39, 232; Henrichs 1993: 36-8; Kerényi 1976: 80, 166, 281-4, 336, 361(note 244), 378, Plates 84-5; Larson 2007: 135-6(Fig. 10.2); Osborne 2007: 251(including Fig. 7.2)-2). Combining both figural elements (the anthropomorphic mask) and non-figural elements (the pole or column), the pole with the mask designated the presence and the power of the deity no less than the betyl (see

Figure 9. Women engaged in ritual activity around a Dionysos mask mounted on a pole. The pole is also adorned with garments and other paraphernalia symbolic of Dionysos. Shown on an Athenian red-figure stamnos by the Villa Giulia Painter, *c*. 450 BC. Height: 47.4 cm; Diameter: 33.4 cm. Museum of Fine Arts, Boston. Gift of Edward Perry Warren. Accession No: 90. 155a. (Photograph © [2017] Museum of Fine Arts, Boston).

3.8 below), the figural statue, and particularly the herm that, like the mask-on-pole, might be considered as a composite, semi-figural monument but of a more durable material, usually marble or stone (Gaifman 2012: 12-3, 36(including Fig. 1.2)-7(Fig. 1.3), 39, 75, 83-4; Simon 1962: 143 quoted in Kerényi 1976: 380. See also Bowden 2010: 135-6).

In a manner similar to the one described immediately above, a deity's symbol, statue / figurine (sometimes housed in a small shrine), or even a representation of its totem animal might also be placed on board a ship to ensure divine guardianship and protection to the ship and to its crew. To maintain the link with their divine protector/s, seafarers were provided with cultic areas – generally, on the prow or on the stern – for worhsip on board the ship. Thus, representations or symbols of protective deities (as well as sacred standards and portable altars) might be mounted on either prow or stern (Figure 10) from where the seafarers could perform rituals in honour of the guardian deity and also to other deities who might have been deemed important for the safety and well being of the crew (Brody 1998: 20, 25-34, 37-8, 61-72, Figs. 16, 18-9, 24, 65-6, 69). It was presumably in this manner that the crew on board the ship carrying the prophet Jonah to Tarshish prayed, offered a sacrifice, and made vows to their gods and to the Lord God of Jonah to relieve them from the storm (Jonah 1: 5, 14, 16). The practice of performing sacrifices on board sea-vessels appears to have known no temporal or cultural boundaries. An early modern witness account by a Christian captive on board a Muslim corsairs' vessel describes the sacrifice of a sheep on the

Figure 10. Standards mounted on poles on a ship depicted on a sacrificial stela from Carthage. The standards carry symbols of Tinnit / Tanit on prow and stern and a caduceus in the middle. (Source: Brody 1998: Fig. 16).

bow of the vessel before attacking a Christian sailing ship (Gambin 2010: 149). And, until today, modern Egyptian boats on the river Nile maintain the tradition of keeping apotropaic symbols (like 'Fatima's Hand') mounted on poles on their prows (Figure 11) to avert dangers on the river or to ensure a successful catch of fish. Therefore, is it equally possible (especially as it comes from a maritime context) that our presumed mask might have been used on board a ship in the manner described above (in respect of ritual masks) to perform rituals in honour of Dionysos in order to secure divine guardianship and protection, perhaps over the wine cargo and, not least, over the crew and ship itself?

If the ship involved was a merchant ship (as any wrecked ships in the area seem to have been on the basis of their discovered contents, mostly amphorae (see 2.3 above)), this presumed Dionysos mask may gain even more significance. As it grew and spread along with the increase in and expansion of commercial viticulture with which it was particularly associated, the cult of Dionysos became important for both religion and trade. Through his cult, therefore, religion and trade stimulated each other. Consequently, through the spread of viticulture and the export of wine, the cult of Dionysos appears to have found itself established amongst various societies where the vine's product was exported to in response to increasing demand (Stanislawski 1975: 428, 443-4. See also Kerényi 1976: 56, 175). It is not at all unexpected, therefore, that introduction of a cult of Dionysos in the Maltese islands might have taken place as early as the introduction (of unknown date), in the same islands, of the vine (and wine) itself (Azzopardi 2014: 284).

Figure 11. Fatima's hand mounted on a pole on a modern Egyptian boat. This modern practice seems to carry forward the tradition of mounting standards with symbols on poles on sea vessels. (Source: shari-chocolatebox.blogspot.com/2011/02/fatimas-protection.html. Accessed: 28-6-2015).

In the ancient Greek world and particularly in Athens, association of Dionysos and of the introduction of his cult with ships (or with seaborne trade) was made manifest in Dionysiac festivals / processions with the involvement of ship cars often carrying an image of Dionysos to recall the introduction, amongst the relative community, of Dionysos' cult shipboard or by way of the sea (Kerényi 1976: 144, 166-72, Plates 56-7, 59A-B; see also 184, 197, 316). The same ship referred to above seems to have been one of several visiting ships (to Xlendi) owned by foreign owners or traders amongst whom Dionysos might have enjoyed preferential worship on account of his close connection with trade (see immediately above). This could have also been one of the ways in which foreign gods (like Dionysos) might have been introduced by foreign traders in the Maltese islands.

Similarly, Egyptian gods were introduced into the western Mediterranean by Egyptian merchants or by merchants who had become familiar with Egyptian gods, as well as by itinerant priests. Initially worshipped in private, these Egyptian gods gradually attracted local communities too and, consequently, went public (Nielsen 2014: 61, 125, 129-30). Having possibly been likewise attracted by newly-introduced gods (like Dionysos), the local people on the Maltese islands might have 'reworked' these gods and assimilated them with their own (as in Nielsen 2014: 30). To take an example from the local Maltese or Gozitan scenario, Dionysos might have been assimilated by the indigenous population with his Punic counterpart Shadrapa amongst whom the latter is likely to have already enjoyed worhsip (see also 3.6, 3.9 below).

Chapter 3

3.1 The toponym 'Ras il-Wardija'

Also met with in connection with other places in Malta and Gozo, the name 'Wardija' is a corruption of the Italian word '*Guardia*' which means 'watch'. Possibly of Medieval origins, the toponym indicates a look-out post or guard station (*MISSIONE 1964*: 167; Zammit Ciantar 2000: 75, 113). All places named 'Wardija' or whose toponyms include 'Wardija' are strategically located on hilltops or promontories from where one could easily watch or guard over the surrounding area or nearby coast.

The toponym 'Ras il-Wardija' is sometimes also indicated in its English version as 'Wardija Point'. '*Ras*' ('point' or 'cape') would refer to the headland on which a look-out post ('*Guardia*' / '*Wardija*') might have once stood. Remains of a tower or signal station dating back to the period of the First World War (1914-8) (*MISSIONE 1967*: 93. See also Buhagiar 2014: 15) are visible to this day on the highest part of Ras il-Wardija. The wide and unobstructed views enjoyed from the promontory would confirm the potential offered by the place for watch purposes. This same visual potential offered by Ras il-Wardija appears to have been exploited in earlier Classical times even if not in direct association with watch practices.

3.2 Origins and development of the sanctuary complex

Without excluding other possible explanations, the proximity of the Xlendi shipwrecks to the Ras il-Wardija promontory (see 2.3 above) where the sanctuary which may have been contemporary to any of the Xlendi wrecks is situated, may suggest a possible link between any of these shipwrecks and the erection or foundation of the mentioned sanctuary on the promontory. Such a possible link might have been either by way of commemoration of the shipwreck (as in Brody 1998: 41, 55, 61), marking a dangerous area (as confirmed by the presence of the nearby shipwrecks) (as in Brody 1998: 41, 55, 61), or setting up a sanctuary in thanksgiving or fulfillment of a vow by any survivors of the wrecked vessel (as in Aulisa 2014: 136; Brody 1998: 48-9, 96, 101). In view of these possibilities, one cannot exclude erection and / or use of the sanctuary by foreign sailors or merchants as the Palmyrene merchants did at Dura-Europos, as the Phoenician merchants did on the Aegean island of

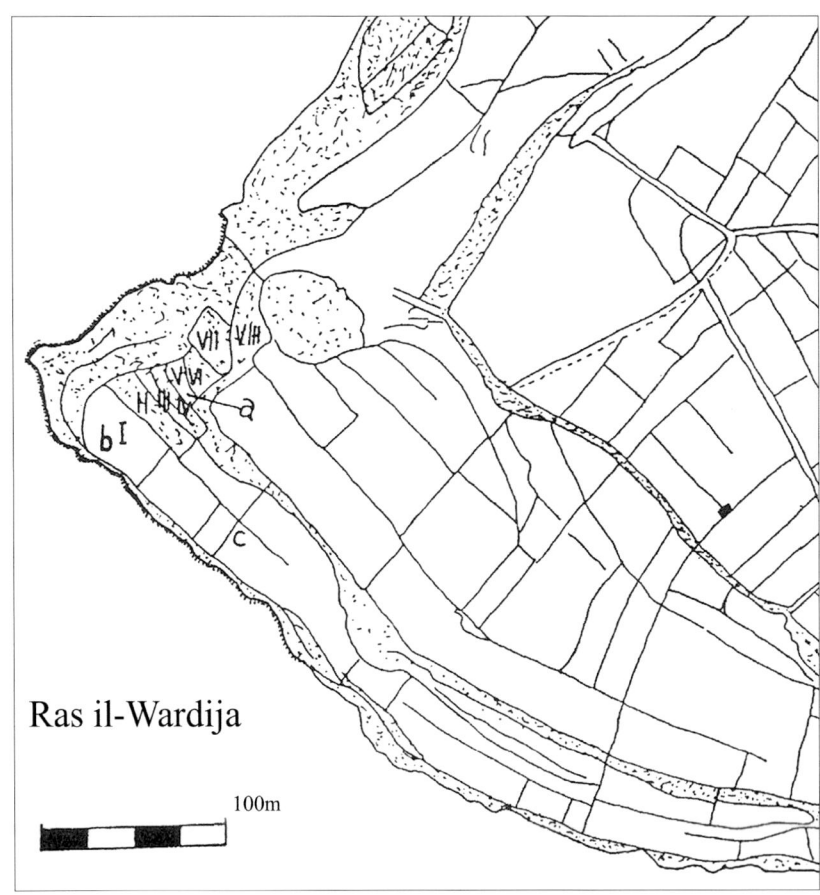

Figure 12. Location map of Ras il-Wardija. The sanctuary's eight terraces are numbered I-VIII on the promontory. (Source: *MISSIONE 1964*: Fig. 11).

Delos and in Italy, or as the Syrian traders did in Rome (Nielsen 2014: 142-9, 151-2), to mention but a few examples.

The sanctuary at Ras il-Wardija is spread on a coastal slope that was terraced apparently in later times (Figure 12), probably for agricultural purposes (*MISSIONE 1966*: 81, 88, 90-1, 123). With the exception of the first and fifth, the other terraces of the sanctuary site did not yield any material evidence either by way of rock-cut features, built structures, or significant amounts of ceramics. The main components of the sanctuary consist of a stone-built quadrangular structure evidently of a cultic nature on the first and lowest terrace (see 3.5 below) and a rock-cut cave with ancillary features on the fifth terrace (see 3.6 below). In view of this, activity at Ras il-Wardija – at least that related to rock-cut or built structures – seems to have been focused on the first and fifth terraces. In association with this activity and on the basis of the excavated ceramic material, use was made of pottery vessels which, in their majority, were apparently in common use during the 3rd-2nd centuries BC. Later activity on the site also employed ceramic vessels of the 1st and 2nd centuries AD; possibly, even of a fourth-century AD date (*MISSIONE 1966*: 123).

To provide access to the sanctuary, the rock surface on the southern boundary of the complex seems to have been adapted to accommodate what appears to have been a ramp leading to the sanctuary's fifth terrace (*MISSIONE 1967*: 92-3, Plates 42(3)-3) but extended to the first terrace as well (*MISSIONE 1964*: 168, 175-6, Plate 83; *1965*: 143-5, Plate 105(1-2)).

Set in a peripheral location in relation to the central cults of Gozo's main urban centre in the heart of the island, the sanctuary did not only mark a liminal space but, with the deployment of architectural features there, this same liminal space was monumentalised. Whatever the reason, the sloping promontory where the sanctuary stands (Figure 13) seems to have been purposely selected. Occupying an area of around 5000 m² and situated on a high promontory, the sanctuary assumes the nature of a 'high place', visually dominating the sea and the adjacent coastline, while itself is quite visible from far out at sea. Although apparently terraced in later times (see above), the sloping profile of the sanctuary may perhaps recall the more magnificent terrace complexes of sanctuaries known from the contemporary Mediterranean world

Figure 13. Ras il-Wardija promontory's sloping profile. The slope is viewed uphill from the first terrace towards the rock-cut cave on the fifth terrace. The temple remains on the first terrace can be seen in the foreground. (Photo: The author).

(see Horsnaes 2002: 233), not least Phoenician ones like those on the Aegean island of Delos (Nielsen 2014: 145-9).

3.3 Relationship between the sanctuary and the physical form of the landscape

Landscapes can be permeated with ritual and religion which means that they may consist, in part (at least), of ritually or spiritually significant places, themselves making up a 'sacred map'. A landscape, on its part, may encompass both anthropogenic and natural features (like streams and hills) which are held as sacred due to the role they play in human experience or the culturally distinct symbols they carry. Permanent natural features (in the landscape) which are held as inherently sacred could be regarded as places of spiritual power, but artificial ones could be also integrated. Landscape features would become, in this way, an embodiment of spiritual forces. These spiritual forces are released through ritual ceremonies aimed at maintaining continuity between the deities, the social group, and the place (Bradley 1991: 135-7; 2000: 28-9, 41-3, 100-4; Crumley 1999: 274; Edmonds 1999: 6; Jost 1994: 217; Kearns 2010: 328; Lahiri 1996: 245-7; Marangou 2001: 153; Mather 2003: 25-6, 32-40; Sahlqvist 2001: 79; Sinopoli 2003: 21; Steinsapir 1999: 182; Valk 2007: 201-10; Zifferero 2002: 255-6). This would entail a transformation of the landscape into not only a meaningful but also a living and dynamic place with its 'actors' (the people) in constant engagement among themselves and with the landscape, having been thus transferred from the domain of wilderness to the domain of humans and culture (enculturation of landscape) through the mediation of the integrated artificial features like monuments (as in Azzopardi 2014: 198-9, 227; Bender 1993: 15).

Coastal landforms, in particular, might sometimes be themselves perceived in the form of a built monument. Alternatively, in the absence of such a landform or perception, an actual monument might be built as a cultural elaboration of the actual landform as might have been the case at Ras il-Wardija. From its prominent location on the impressive promontory, the Ras il-Wardija sanctuary might have been a natural landmark for sailors (see 3.4 below). The significance of the sanctuary might have been further enhanced by the use of building material probably quarried from its immediate surroundings (see 3.5 below) to the extent that it might have blended with its geological and topographical surroundings. Therefore, in using local building materials in such a visible manner, a powerful resonance might have been established between the built sanctuary and its local setting. The integration of the sanctuary in the natural setting of the Ras il-Wardija promontory might have also invested the former with some of the special qualities of the latter. The building of the sanctuary on that particular promontory might have also been intended to highlight an aspect which was seen as inherent in that landscape (as in Scarre 2002: 9-10).

Because of their superior position and awe-inspiring character, high places have always impressed humanity (Tilley 2004: 6) and, thus, were often monumentalised. High and prominent places like hills or mountains were, in fact, amongst the commonest places chosen for religious monuments and rituals (Briault 2007: 123). The dominant location of the Ras il-Wardija sanctuary high on a visually impressive promontory seems to highlight a specific symbolic relationship between the sanctuary itself and the natural rock formation on which it stands. The association of the sanctuary with the visually impressive promontory may have been particularly significant. The sanctuary was meant to be seen, approached, and visited for ritual activities. The construction of the sanctuary, therefore, may have helped to establish a material and enduring relationship between the ritual practices and the landscape with its topographical features. In this way, the topographic space became also incorporated in the construction of the sanctuary and, making the sanctuary visible, may have enabled it to draw power from the landscape to exert ritual control (as in Tilley 1996: 167).

Moreover, the construction of artificial features in a landscape might be a form of ordering, management, control, and domestication of that landscape through its conversion brought about also by the incorporation in it of architectural orders, thus bringing external spiritual forces into the domain of human society. Monumentalisation of spiritually significant natural landscapes via the construction or insertion of artificial or architectural features may enrich them with additional symbolism, imbue them with more significance and new meanings, and formalise their use. Then, through its reservation for ritual and its consequent and conscious separation from human settlements, the land is defined while, through the ritual mechanism itself, it continues to be domesticated (Bradley 1991: 139; 2000: 107-13, 158; Guettel Cole 1994: 216; Harding 1991: 146-7; Mather 2003: 27, 29, 36, 40-1; Parcero Oubina *et al.* 1998: 173; Prent 2003: 87, 89; Steinsapir 1999: 189, 192; Valk 2007: 209).

With their building of the sanctuary complex down the natural coastal slope at Ras il-Wardija, the people responsible for it might have been seeking to formalise, materialise, and make explicit a symbolic relationship between the landscape they knew of and themselves as a (religious) community. On similar lines, the construction of the sanctuary might have also highlighted another symbolic relationship between the sanctuary itself and the naturally sloping landscape. At the same time, the construction of the sanctuary complex down the natural coastal slope may have emphasised the cultural significance of the naturally contoured landscape. In so doing, the construction of the sanctuary also established a material, tangible, and enduring relationship between the ritual practices enacted there and the landscape, while freezing the latter in time (as in Tilley 1996: 167).

The first and fifth terraces may have provided the stage for the main activities like worship, dining, and gatherings undertaken at the sanctuary (see 3.5-6, 3.8-9 below). The rest of the terraces, on the other hand, might have provided the stage for subsidiary activities like processions (see 3.6 below). The manipulation and development of the natural contours might have been intended not only to create formal surfaces accommodating activities but also to cater for a growing number of people. The latter might bring to the fore the possibility of social differentiation both in terms of access to certain spaces and also in the overall use of space (as in Morgan 1994: 125-6).

The basin or pool on the fifth terrace may have also been integral to the experience of the sanctuary site on account of any rites – like purification and / or initiation rites – it may have been associated with. And, through the enacted rituals, processions, and possible pilgrimages, this experience of the sanctuary site itself may have also extended into that of the surrounding landscape (as in Ghey 2007: 26).

3.4 Visual domination of the seascape

Like other Mediterranean communities, those on the Maltese islands must have experienced the sea as a constantly changing dynamic medium. For them, the sea was also a giver and a taker of life and, thus, it is likely to have been perceived by them as imbued with spiritual essences, energies, or forces that form its dynamic character. Maltese and Gozitan coastal sanctuaries, and the headland ones in particular, were liminal zones where the land meets the sea. As such, they were ideal places for human spiritual relationships and engagements with the sea or with its spiritual forces. As the sea (or its spiritual forces) is to be tamed and dominated in order to facilitate sea travel and exploitation of marine resources, the ritual performance the Maltese and Gozitan communities enacted at these specifically-located sanctuaries allowed spiritual management and control of the sea, of the seascapes, and of their spiritual forces more effectively. These rituals further inscribed the seascapes with prescribed liminal zones where the spiritual could be experienced through bodily or sensual engagement. The rituals may have included offerings aimed at placating the sea's spiritual forces and ensure safe travel (McNiven 2003: 329-44 for comparisons).

The maritime environment of coastal areas – be they part of islands or mainlands – with their characteristics like pronounced promontories and sheltered inlets seems bound to be impregnated with the divine. This may be explained in view of the way these places are often perceived and in view of the significance which, as a consequence, is attached to them. Such places, therefore, would become the focus of religious worship where deities with maritime connections are not simply venerated but, more importantly, invoked for their aid and refuge. This would, in turn, continue to enhance the places' religious significance (Azzopardi 2014: 92).

For this reason, coastal areas were often not lacking in sacred character. Sacred places along the coastlines or linked to harbours not only protected these and their associated communities, but also underlined the coastlines' status as the border where land, sea, and sky met (Scarre 2002: 9). Coastal promontories (or headlands) share a number of characteristics with high places besides their relation to the sea. Viewed from the sea, they are impressive, prominent, and conspicuous landmarks which might create a feeling of proximity to the gods (Malkin 1987: 142, 146-8). Acting also as distinct coastal features, they could be used as 'seamarks' in locating land and identifying coastal positions from the sea. Very often, they would serve this role better if they are defined by a structure. This is often of a religious nature. This structure defines a space, sometimes separated from the hinterland by a built boundary but, for its remaining extent, surrounded by the sea. Headland structures, therefore, may have been purposely positioned and defined so as to create a symbolic link between the land and the sea (Figure 14). In this way, more than simply providing key landmarks in aid of mariners, promontories or headlands also provided a liminal zone where people of the sea and those of the littoral could come together (Rainbird 2007: 55-6, 159-60). Thus, coastal or harbour shrines (or sanctuaries) allowed contact between the local community and external traders and sailors frequenting them (i.e. the shrines or sanctuaries) on their safe arrival. This cultural mix is frequently manifested by way of the richness and complexity of non-local cultural features evident in coastal shrines or sanctuaries (Zifferero 2002: 262).

The importance for seafarers, in particular, of the pantheon of different gods and goddesses with maritime associations is, in fact, also best shown by the presence of coastal or seaside worshipping spaces. Sanctuaries and shrines located in or next to harbours or on headlands and dedicated to such guardian deities acted as sacral focal points for seafarers to help them maintain their link to their divine guardians and protectors both in harbour and at sea (Brody 1998: 38, 61, 84-5, 99-100. See also Aulisa 2014: 140).

Thus, headlands or promontories might be connected with a deity who would be protector of those who sailed within sight of that headland or promontory. The visibility of the headland or promontory could have also

Figure 14. Ras ir-Raheb promontory (in Malta) from the air. To create a symbolic link between the land and the sea, a temple structure (arrowed) was purposely positioned on the prominent and conspicuous promontory. (Photograph © Daniel Cilia).

facilitated the identification of that same headland or promontory as a landmark and navigational reference for mariners and fishermen. Erection of a temple (or an altar) on that headland or promontory like those at Ras ir-Raħeb in Malta and at Ras il-Wardija in Gozo (and, likewise, in harbours) might have served to thank the deity and to ensure the safety of the seafarers. And if the seafarers could not stop to pay their homage at these temples or shrines, they could pray to the resident god from their vessel at sea and within sight of the promontory temple or shrine. This would have, thus, confirmed the importance of that deity as the seafarers' guardian and the importance of the headland or promontory (or harbour) itself for the seafarers (Brody 1998: 21-4, 33-41, 55, 61, 81, 85, 99, 101). In assertion of the latter's importance, it is perhaps worth pointing out that grottos or promontories (both of which are also to be found at Ras il-Wardija) may also themselves constitute natural 'sanctuaries' where humans could perceive divine presence and power (as in Aulisa 2014: 144).

Usually isolated from settlements along the coast, shrines built on seaside promontories did not simply link the seafarers to their patron deities but, visible from the sea, they maintained the seafarers' link to their divine guardians and protectors even while away from their home port. Nautical expeditions could also lead to the discovery of previously unknown promontories and their eventual dedication to seafarers' patron deities. The foundation and dedication of a temple to the Semitic 'Poseidon' on a wooded promontory by the Carthaginian captain Hanno during a colonising sea voyage along the Atlantic coast of Africa reflects this Phoenician practice of commemorating newly-found headlands. Furthermore, shrines on seaside promontories could also mark particularly dangerous areas along the sea journey, provide a sighting or a landmark to aid navigation from the sea (see above), mark freshwater sources where ships could stop to replenish their water supplies, or commemorate an event like a battle or a shipwreck (Brody 1998: 37-41, 55-61, 81, 96-101).

Considering its altitude and extreme exposure to natural elements, particularly the winds, the Ras il-Wardija site cannot be imagined to have attracted any permanent settlements. Nor did any permanent settlements in its immediate surroundings seem to have been intended (see 3.10 below). Yet, due to its particular location, it does not only mark a liminal space forming a boundary between land and sea (see below and 3.2 above), but it also dominates the seascape (Figure 15) from where it can be seen for miles around. It seems, therefore, that visibility – and, specifically, visibility from the sea – was a crucial factor in the choice of the sanctuary location.

Another factor which may have contributed towards the visibility of the sanctuary site could have been its

Figure 15. Ras il-Wardija dominating the seascape. The promontory's dominant position provides it with a view of the open sea for miles around. (Photo: The author).

possible monumentality. If the sanctuary was meant to be seen, especially from far out at sea, its possible monumentality not only dominated the sanctuary's seascape but also rendered the sanctuary site more visible (as in Bradley 2000: 106). As it towered over the surrounding sea, the sanctuary must have been a distinctive and highly visible feature marking the presence of the gods to those sailing around (as in Sinopoli 2003: 25) or extending divine presence to the sea (as in Azzopardi 2014: 296). And as visual experiences are crucial to the experience of place (Van Dyke and Alcock 2003: 6), the sanctuary appears to have been meant to be seen in order to be eventually visited.

But apart from enabling the sanctuary site to be seen from far out at sea, another factor, namely the significant height of the cliffs on which the sanctuary itself stands, seems to reflect the earth-heavens cosmic axis. This height renders the sanctuary on top of the cliffs not only awe-inspiring and visually impressive but, perhaps more significantly, it relates the sanctuary to the skies towards which it (i.e. the height of the cliffs) points up. As they are the domain of the spirit powers, the skies always tend to be culturally and emotionally privileged (Tilley 2004: 6). Simultaneously, as they project up towards the skies, high places are sometimes viewed as links or entry points to the supernatural world (Crumley 1999: 272) or as points of contact between heaven and earth (Bradley 2000: 26-7). Thus, on a more particular note, the high location of the sanctuary would have also brought the worshippers into closer relationship with the heavenly deities.

Nonetheless, the evidently preferred location for the construction of the Ras il-Wardija sanctuary may have borne out the latter's direct connection with the sea even more. Having been apparently preferred to the higher – and, therefore, more conspicuous – hillock behind it, the coastal slope where the sanctuary was constructed (and where it could still be seen, even from far out at sea) brought the sanctuary physically closer to the sea. In so doing, it also underscored the liminal character of the sanctuary serving as a boundary between land and sea.

As at Ras ir-Raħeb in Malta with which it enjoyed visual links (Figure 16. See also Azzopardi 2014: 202-3(Fig. 45), 249), the coastal location of the Ras ir-Wardija sanctuary could also indicate the attitudes of the associated community towards the sea. As the sanctuary could be seen from the sea but not so much from the hinterland until one got close, it seems to have been an outward looking society as, perhaps, might have been expected from an island society and as, indeed, was to happen in Malta even in later times (Stoddart 1999: 144). Also notable in this respect is the east-west alignment of the sanctuary similar to that of the one on the Ras ir-Raħeb promontory in Malta whereby entry into both sanctuaries was oriented seawards: a phenomenon which might have borne certain significance perhaps out of their respective associations with the sea (Azzopardi 2014: 248-9).

Figure 16. Ras il-Wardija viewed from Ras ir-Raħeb (in Malta) across the channel. The two sanctuaries on the respective promontories enjoyed a visual link. (Photo: The author).

But the coast was often also a marginal

area located outside the sphere of normal domestic life because it was situated on an edge of the settled land, a place where opposites met, where earth met the sea, or where the world of the living humans came in contact with the depths of the non-human 'world' of the sea. Moreover, the sea not only provided marine foods, maritime communication, and a living, but was also often perceived as full of risks and dangers that threatened human life. Consequently, the coast (and, sometimes, even the ship itself) was also a sacred or ritual place where, amongst other rituals, one could offer sacrifices or make offerings before undertaking a perilous journey; or else, offer thanksgiving following return from such a journey (Aulisa 2014: 123-7, 129, 136-7; Bradley 2000: 27; Scarre 2002: 9. Also as in Aulisa 2014: 134-5, 137-8, 143-4; Galdi 2014: 149-51, 161).

Nevertheless, all the above would show that the significance of seascapes is likely to have gone beyond that of mere subsistence strategies. Seascapes attained a religious significance highlighted with the establishment of liminal zones marked by the establishment of coastal sanctuaries. Located by the edge of a coastal cliff where the land meets the sea, the Ras il-Wardija sanctuary is a good example of a liminal sanctuary. But apart from creating horizontal links between land (including people) and sea, it also created vertical links between sky and earth, between deities and communities (see Azzopardi 2014: 297-8).

3.5 The temple building on the first terrace

The first and lowest terrace, near the cliff edge, hosted what appears to have been a quadrangular structure (Figure 17) identified by its excavators as a temple (see below). Its surviving remains occupy an area of around 169 m² and do not reach any higher than one or two stone courses. Built of dry Globigerina stone blocks cut in various forms and dimensions, this temple structure was orientated east-west with its entrance's surviving threshold facing east (*MISSIONE 1964*: 173-4, Fig. 13, Plates 80-2; *1966*: 95-6, Fig. 13, Plates 63-7).

No traces of any further extensions of this temple were found. Nor is it clear how it was roofed or whether it was roofed or not (*MISSIONE 1966*: 100); although the fact that it was plastered (see below) would indicate that it was roofed. This would seem to be further confirmed by the fact that the surviving plaster fragments do not bear any patina resulting from exposure to natural elements. Furthermore, had it been roofless, there would have been hardly any scope for closing the temple's door as suggested by pivot hinge sockets on the door's surviving threshold (*MISSIONE 1964*: 174, Fig. 13, Plate 81(1)). Judging by the surviving remains and dimensions of its structure (see above), this temple seems to have been of a simple quadrangular plan or single room plan, perhaps like the temples of Demeter at Eretria and Corinth (Gaifman 2012: 134). Other temples which may have looked somewhat similar with their broadly quadrangular plan and dimensions are the so-called 'archaic temple' (Figure 18) attributed to Tanit by Ferruccio Barreca (Pesce 2000: 219) on Capo San Marco and the small Punic temple (Figure 19) on the *isolotto di Su Cardolinu* at Chia (ancient Bithia), both in Sardegna and both of which survive only in ruins.

Unless it represents a later activity, evidence of stone extraction encountered on the first terrace where the temple is to be found (*MISSIONE 1965*: 145-7, Plates 105(1, 3)-7(1)) could indicate that the stones for the building of the temple may have been sourced from the immediate vicinity. This might have been also the case in respect of Temple B at Kommos in Crete, the ashlar blocks of which seem to have been quarried from its surrounding cult area (Shaw and Shaw 2000: 24 cited in Prent 2003: 87). Stone blocks for the building of the temple on the Ras ir Raheb promontory on the western coast of Malta might have also been supplied from nearby old quarries (Azzopardi 2014: 42, 193-4, 201; Buhagiar 2014: 15) that are visible to this day. Extracting the building material (like stone) for a monument from its own location or surrounding landscape might help to integrate the monument more firmly within its surrounding natural setting (Azzopardi 2014: 42).

In spite of numerous fragments of ancient floors found both inside and beyond the temple (at Ras il-Wardija), the excavators believe that these should have belonged to another non-surviving structure but

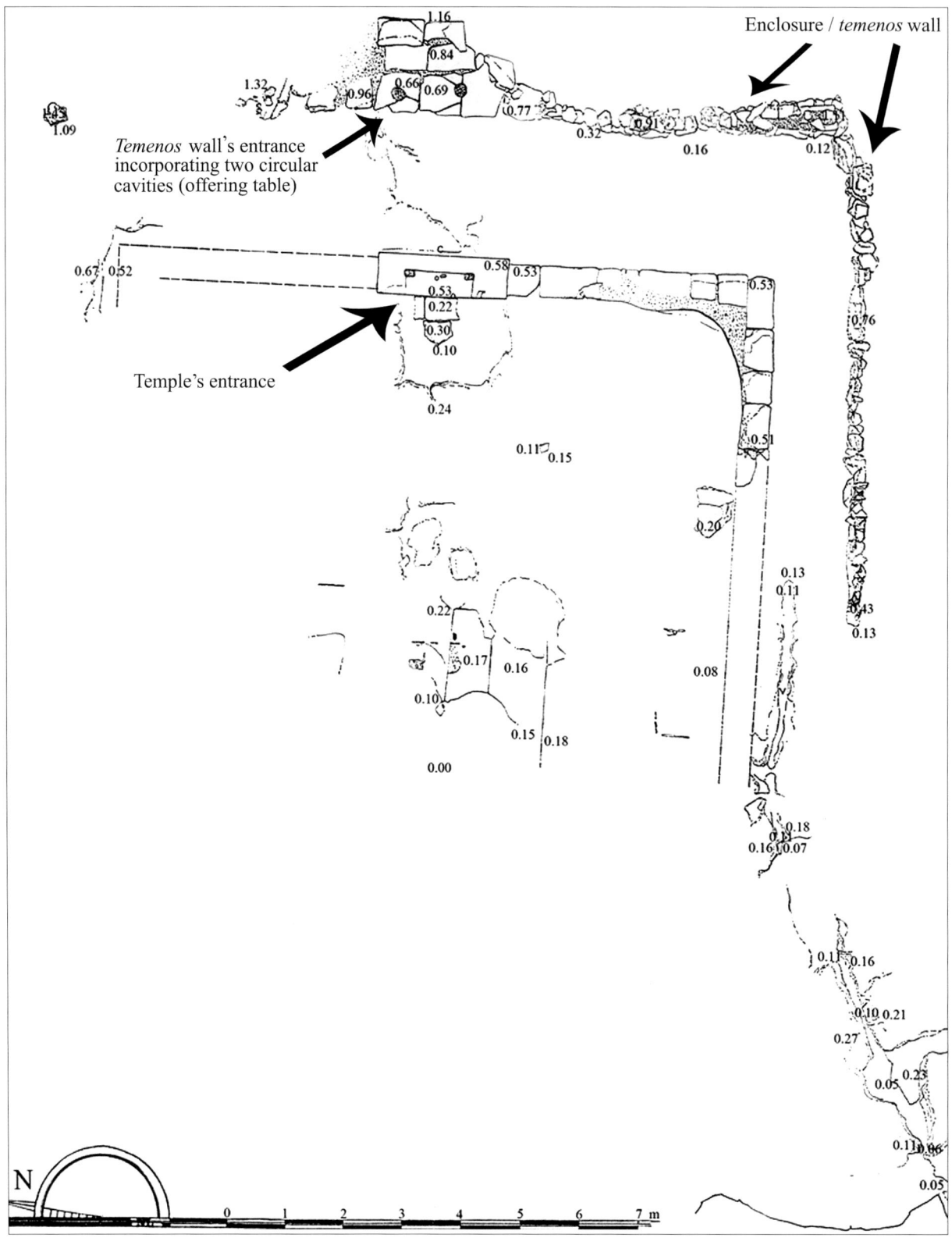

Figure 17. Plan of the temple remains. These are to be found on the first terrace of the sanctuary complex. Level readings are given in metres at various points on the plan. (After *MISSIONE 1967*: Fig. 9).

not to this particular one (*MISSIONE 1965*: 148-51, Plate 107(2); *1966*: 106; *1967*: 92). Rather, it is the relatively flat rock surface that appears to have served as a natural floor both inside and outside the temple structure and it was only levelled wherever it was felt necessary (*MISSIONE 1966*: 82, 94, 96-8, 106, Plates 64-5). This is sustained by traces of burning visible on the rock surface as a result of its direct contact with fire, a number of cuts directly in bedrock, and remnants of plaster that appear to have covered walls or standing features / structures but, at the same time, were in direct contact with bedrock (*MISSIONE 1964*: 175; *1966*: 97, 103, 105-7, Fig. 13, Plate 70(1-2)).

Figure 18. The so-called 'archaic temple' on Capo San Marco, Sardegna. (Photo: The author).

Both its internal and external wall surfaces seem to have been covered with fine plaster as fragments of this were found both inside and outside what remained of the temple structure (*MISSIONE 1964*: 173-5; *1966*: 96-100, 104-5, Plates 70-1, 75(1); *1967*: 89-90). This would give the impression of a properly treated – and, hence, important – building. Nevertheless, as the plaster was found to have been of two kinds (*MISSIONE 1964*: 173) and, in places, was found in two layers (*MISSIONE 1966*: 105), this would seem to suggest that the building underwent restoration or

Figure 19. The small Punic temple on the *isolotto di Su Cardolinu* at Chia (ancient Bithia), Sardegna. (Photo: The author).

structural renewal and re-plastering at a second stage. To this second stage may have belonged the smaller stones, particularly those employed on the internal side of the building that were covered with plaster similar to plaster found also in fragments in front of the cave on the fifth terrace (*MISSIONE 1964*: 172, 174, Plate 82(3)).

The restoration / structural renewal and re-plastering of the temple building might have been necessitated by a fire which the building might have sustained. This seems to be evidenced not only by the traces of burning on the natural rock floor (see above) but also by remains of ashes found inside (*MISSIONE 1964*: 175) and, perhaps more clearly, by traces of ashes visible on the rear side of plaster fragments detached from the structure's surviving walls and by signs of burning on the stone blocks from where the same plaster fragments were detached. This plaster may have replaced an earlier destroyed plaster. According to the site's excavators, this (renewed) plaster seems to be of Roman date (*MISSIONE 1966*: 97).

On its outside, the temple's quadrangular structure was surrounded by a poorly surviving wall (Figure 17). This wall assumed the appearance of an enclosure / *temenos* wall (Punic: *haràm*) with its own surviving entrance's threshold also facing east and in front of the temple's entrance (*MISSIONE 1966*: 102-3, Fig. 13, Plates 64-5, 67(2), 73(1)). Built in a rustic technique, employing variously sized and differently shaped natural stones, the wall formed a sort of a corridor running around the temple's structure (*MISSIONE 1967*: 87-9, Fig. 9, Plates 38-9). The space created by this corridor also yielded fragments of plaster (*MISSIONE 1966*: 105). As inside the temple, the floor of this corridor was likewise provided by the regular surface of the natural bedrock (*MISSIONE 1966*: 103, Plate 73). The wall's rustic technique would rather suggest a shallow wall (*MISSIONE 1967*: 88).

The presence of a *temenos* wall surrounding the temple may have recalled the more typically Greek tradition of a *temenos* including a temple housing the deity, whether in figural or aniconic form (Gaifman 2012: 134). With its surrounding *temenos* wall, our temple may be also somewhat likened to the poorly surviving Punic temple at Menzel Harb in Tunisia (Foucher 1966: 123(plan). See also *MISSIONE 1966*: 124; *1967*: 104).

Significantly, the threshold of the *temenos* wall's entrance incorporated two circular cavities (Figure 17). This particular threshold arrangement finds a close parallel in similar examples encountered in some Maltese prehistoric temples which might betray an earlier tradition of the same practice (see also 3.7 below). In view of this, this set of two cavities and three other similar sets located on the fifth terrace (see 3.6 below) led the site's excavators to identify here offering tables with cavities or holes evidently meant to take offerings. The presence of the presumed offering table forming part of the threshold of the enclosure / *temenos* wall's entrance and thus in close association with the quadrangular structure further led the excavators to attribute a cultic nature to the latter, identifying it as a temple (*MISSIONE 1966*: 100-2, Fig. 13, Plates 72-3(2), 67(2)-8(1); *1967*: 87-9, Fig. 9, Plate 38(1)).

The presumed offering table, which will be the object of further discussion in 3.7 below, was aligned with both temple's entrance (which also faced east) and, further beyond, also with a nearly centrally located levelled-out space on the natural rock floor inside the said temple (*MISSIONE 1967*: 88, Fig. 9). This levelled-out space might have accommodated an altar-like platform or support (possibly, also plastered) (*MISSIONE 1966*: 97-8, Fig. 13, Plate 70(1-2); *1967*: 90, Fig. 9, Plate 40(2)) which might have held a stone pyramidal betyl (discussed in 3.8 below) found between the outer wall of the temple and the enclosure / *temenos* wall and not far from the latter's entrance's threshold (with its offering table) and from that of the temple (*MISSIONE 1966*: 104, Plate 75(3-4)). This pyramidal betyl might have, therefore, received offerings on the offering table in front. Taken together, these considerations would further qualify the quadrangular structure as a cultic building or temple associated with some form or forms of worship whilst the deployment of this sort of architecture on the rocky promontory would have marked the latter as a locus of divine presence (as in Gaifman 2012: 157, 161-3).

Whilst extending the excavation on the first terrace towards the cliff edge in an attempt to uncover any surviving structural remains (whether separate from or forming part of the temple), the excavators came across three significant stones. Two were actually fragments of stone mouldings that raised the excavators' suspicion as to whether they formed part of an altar or altars (*MISSIONE 1965*: 151, Plate 107(3); *1966*: 104, Plate 75(2)). But even if they did, it is difficult to determine whether they belonged to the temple or to any other non-surviving sacred structures on the same terrace. Likewise can be said with respect to another stone. This was a slab of large dimensions. According to the excavators, it is likely to have been a stela but was not in situ. However, what struck the excavators' attention were a number of pickaxe marks especially on its central part, leading one to suspect an intentional defacement to the stone (*MISSIONE 1967*: 91-2, 104, Fig. 9, Plate 42(1-2)). Had it been intentional (as the excavators themselves also suspected), did this mutilation mark the termination of a cult associated with the stone or the ritual closure of the sanctuary (as in Glinister 2000: 69-70)? At any rate, the stone (or the presumed stela) was maintained within the sacred precinct presumably on account of its sacred character, while its mutilation would have prevented its reuse (as in Glinister 2000: 56-60, 67-70).

With its verticality or upright shape, a standing slab or stone (like the presumed stela mentioned immediately above) could have been able to set apart a specific space and, thus, could have also served as a spatial marker (Gaifman 2012: 181-2, 185, 202). Demarcating a space, it could have also asserted human intervention (Gaifman 2012: 185). But when it designates a space in a religious context, the upright stone would normally assume the role of constructing or marking the physical limits of a divinity's space or the space belonging to a deity and, in so doing, it signals the deity's potential divine presence (Gaifman 2012: 181-2, 184). As the stone in question was not found in situ (see above), it might prove difficult to determine its true function. Nonetheless, the stone's shape and the religious context in which it was ultimately found might serve as indicators which are not to be ignored either.

As on the rest of the first terrace and the remaining terraces of the sanctuary, most of the pottery found both inside the temple as well as in its immediate vicinity (including the space between the temple and the *temenos* wall) was unstratified, perhaps as a result of agricultural activity in later times. Yet it was homogenous and, like the plaster fragments, must have belonged to the temple (*MISSIONE 1967*: 94). The ceramic repertoire from the temple itself and from its immediate vicinity consisted of Punic pottery, Roman pottery, and pottery betraying Roman forms but worked and decorated in Punic tradition. Its chronological range covered a time span from the 3rd or 2nd century BC to the 1st or 2nd century AD, possibly even as late as the 4th century AD, with occasional fragments of a Mediaeval date (*MISSIONE 1964*: 175; *1965*: 149; *1966*: 108-11, 123, Fig. 14). This would seem to confirm the Punic origins of the temple and its continuous use in Roman times when it was restored / structurally renewed (*MISSIONE 1964*: 176) as suggested by evidence provided by the plaster fragments (see above).

3.6 The cave and ancillary features on the fifth terrace

Further up, a quadrangular room measuring 5.60m by 4.60m was cut into the rock-face overlooking the fifth terrace. This room or artificial cave was orientated east-west, with its entrance facing the sea to the west. A number of features were cut into the walls and on the floor inside the room. A rock-cut U-shaped 'bench' and 'pavement' ran along the three walls of the room, leaving a passage in the middle and orientated towards the room's entrance. In addition, five large niches were cut into its three walls and were surmounted with features in imitation of architectural mouldings (Figure 20). Niche 3 seems to have been surmounted by a tympanum while the remaining four niches appear to have been surmounted by a horizontal entablature (*MISSIONE 1964*: 168-9, Figs. 12-3, Plates 73-5; *1965*: 126, 128-30, Figs. 8-9, Plates 75, 77-9(1), 81-2, 85). These mouldings are hardly visible any longer as a result of the extent of erosion suffered by the internal rock surfaces of the room.

Three schematic figures – two cruciform and one in 'flying' attitude – were also carved on the internal walls of the room. The most distinctive of the two cruciform ones was centrally carved on the internal wall of niche 5 (*MISSIONE 1964*: 169, Plate 75(1); *1965*: 127, Plate 83(3)). Two side-cuts running the whole depth of this niche at mid-height may have accommodated a shelf beneath the cruciform figure (Figure 21) where offerings could have been placed in front of the representation (Figure 53). Similarly-located cuts of a similar kind are visible in the remaining niches too. The cruciform figure in niche 5 was later detached and stolen but is, now, displayed in the Gozo Archaeology Museum, following its recovery. Two other figures, one in 'flying' attitude (Figure 22) and a second cruciform one (Figure 23), were respectively located on wall A, between niches 1 and 2, and on wall C, on the left side of niche 5. The latter rested on

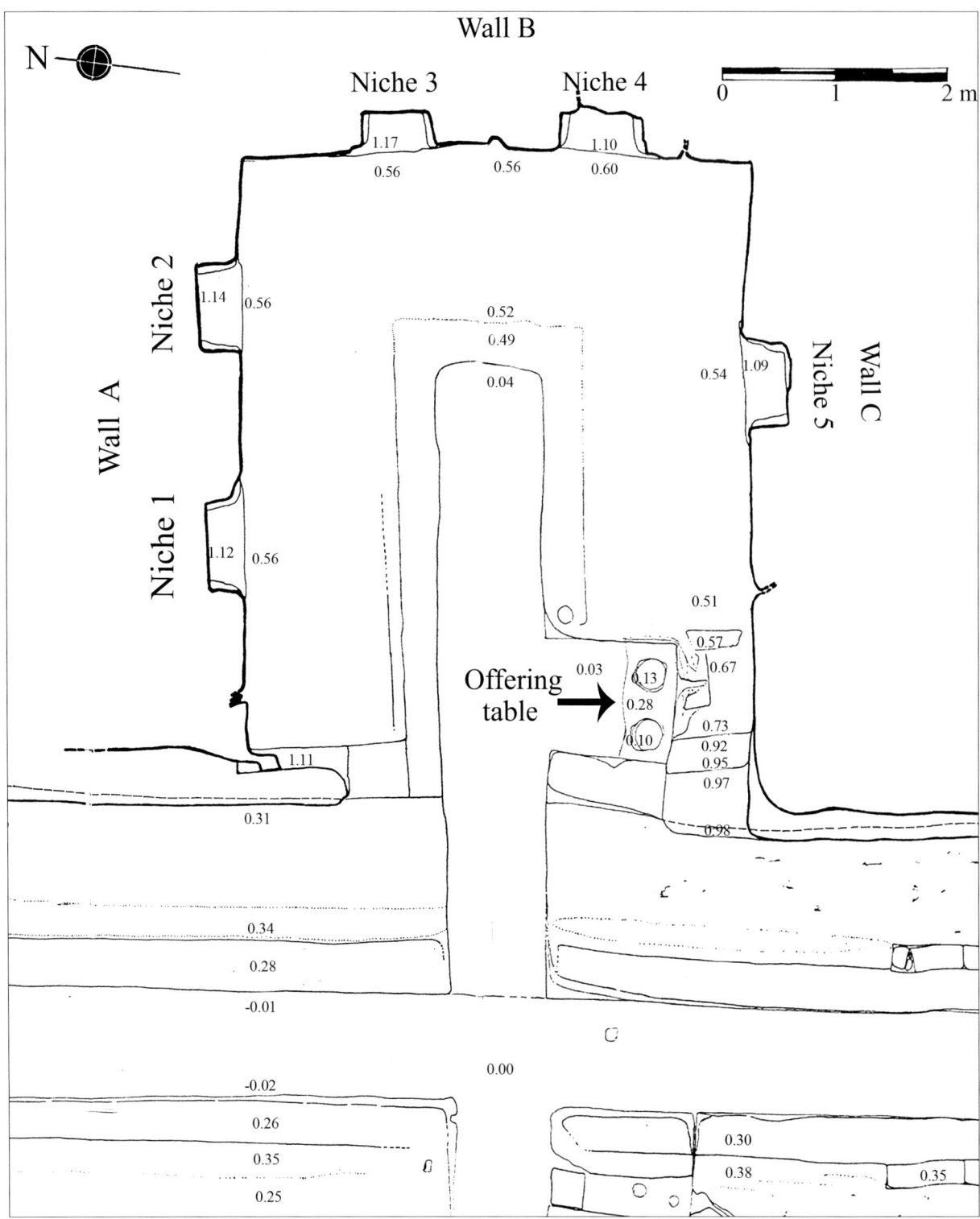

Figure 20. Plan of the rock-cut cave. The cave is to be found on the fifth terrace and has an internal U-shaped bench. Different levels are given in metres at various points on the plan. (After *MISSIONE* 1965: Fig. 8).

top of another carved, yet different (perhaps, also 'flying'?), figure (*MISSIONE* 1965: 126, Plate 83(1-2)). These figures are hardly visible any longer. Their possible significance will be discussed in 3.9 below.

As suggested by what appear to be remnants of a rock-cut screening wall on both northern and southern flanks of the present cave's entrance (*MISSIONE* 1965: 128-9, Fig. 8, Plates 75, 77, 78(2)-81, 84-5), the latter

Figure 21. Niche 5 inside the rock-cut cave. A cruciform figure was centrally carved on the niche's internal wall. Two side-cuts that may have accommodated a shelf beneath the cruciform figure are also visible. (Source: *MISSIONE 1964*: Plate 75(1)).

Figure 22. Figure in 'flying' attitude. It was carved on wall A, between niches 1 and 2 inside the rock-cut cave. (Source: *MISSIONE 1965*: Plate 83(1)).

Figure 23. Small cruciform figure (arrowed) shown on top of a 'flying'(?) figure. It was carved on wall C, on the left side of niche 5 inside the rock-cut cave. (Source: *MISSIONE 1965*: Plate 83(2)).

seems to have been originally screened off, leaving access through a door in the middle. The space between the flanking remnants of the presumed screening wall suggests a doorway nearly 3 m wide. An idea of the presumed original facade and entrance of the cave might, perhaps, be gleaned from those of the rock-cut *triclinium* of Aslah at Petra, in Jordan, as they can be still seen today and where the *triclinium*'s entrance is 2.98m wide (Wenning and Gorgerat 2014: 2(Fig. 3), 5-6 (including Fig. 6), 9(Fig. 8)). Our presumed rock-cut screening wall seems to have been later removed when a roofed structure was presumably built in front of and in extension to the cave (see below). Prior to the last-mentioned intervention, the cave opened onto the fifth terrace which may have acted as a forecourt in relation to the cave. In sanctuaries, this was a feature typical of caves (Nielsen 2014: 141; see also 142 where a similar forecourt included also water installations like the fifth terrace at Ras il-Wardija (see below)).

An offering table similar to the one encountered on the *temenos*' threshold in front of the temple on the first terrace was located by the room's original (and present) entrance and on the latter's southern side. It had two conical cavities while a quadrangular rock-cut platform was cut on its rear (Figure 20). This platform could have held a cult object in front of which offerings could have been placed in the conical cavities on the offering table (*MISSIONE 1965*: 128-9, Fig. 8, Plates 79-80). The possible significance of this rock-cut offering table's location next to the room's original entrance will be discussed in 3.7 below.

The passage inside the room / cave extended outside and beyond the room's entrance where it perpendicularly intersected a (presently) external passage flanked by what the excavators termed as rock-cut 'pavements' and 'benches' on both of its sides and running parallel to the room's facade (Figure 24). The last-mentioned external passage was intersected almost at its centre inasmuch as the room itself was likewise cut almost in the middle of the rock-face (*MISSIONE 1964*: 171-2, Fig. 12, Plates 76, 78; *1965*: 127-33, 165, 178, Fig. 8, Plates 75, 81, 85-93). What looked to be typically Punic mortar was noted in the southernmost extent of this 'pavement' and 'bench' arrangement but very fine plaster fragments surviving in other places along the same 'pavement' and 'bench' arrangement would suggest a Roman period restoration (*MISSIONE 1965*: 132).

The site's excavators expressed the opinion that the (presently) external passage with its arrangement of 'pavements' and 'benches' might have accommodated processions (perhaps even dancing) along its length. According to the excavators, the passage's narrow width could have restricted the procession participants (or dancers) to proceed one after the other in a single row, while the 'benches' and the 'pavements' may have accommodated spectators: seated on the 'benches' and others standing on the 'pavements' behind (*MISSIONE 1965*: 165-7, 178-9).

But the surviving plaster fragments do not bear any patina resulting from exposure to natural elements. Therefore, as in the case of the temple building on the first terrace (see 3.5 above), this fine plaster

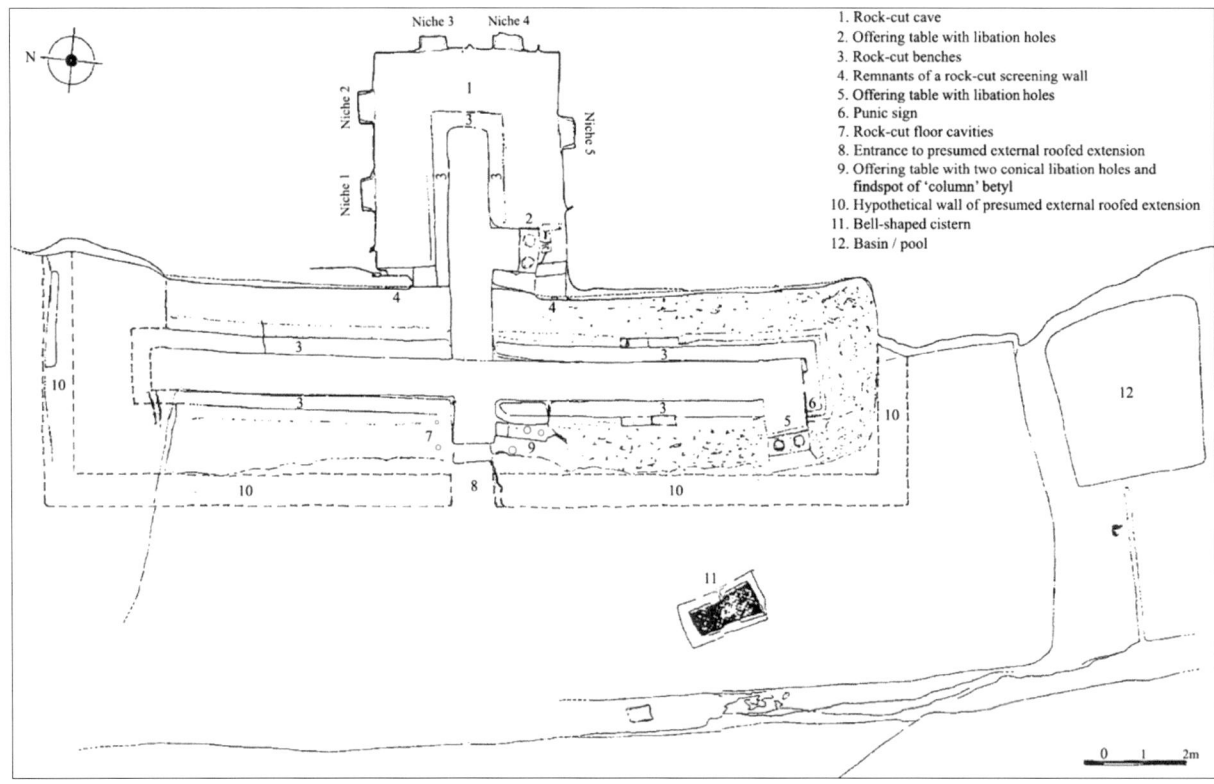

Figure 24. General plan of the rock-cut cave in relation to the external features on the fifth terrace.
(After Buhagiar 2014: 318(Plate 19); *MISSIONE 1965*: Fig. 8).

would seem to suggest that the area extending beyond the cave was covered by a roofed structure (see also below) which was also internally plastered while a similar restoration programme as that on the first-terrace temple building was also undertaken – perhaps, simultaneously – on this presumed built structure. Thus, the surviving plaster would seem to confirm that these passages with their flanking 'pavements' and 'benches' might have not been external at all but, as was even initially suspected by the excavators themselves (*MISSIONE 1964*: 172), could have been accommodated within a built (and roofed) structure which does no longer survive (Figure 24). The Roman date assigned to the plaster by the excavators (*MISSIONE 1964*: 172; *1965*: 132) would indicate the period when this presumed structure was restored (see above) and, thus, already in use. The stones for this same structure may have been sourced from the fifth terrace itself and / or from the adjacent fourth and third terraces as suggested by signs of stone extraction on these same terraces (Figure 25. See also below).

Figure 25. Marks of stone extraction on the third terrace. (Source: *MISSIONE 1966*: Plate 61(2)).

A striking parallel to our rock-cut room or artificial cave on the fifth terrace is provided by the cult caves in the sanctuary of Poseidon near the Isthmus of Corinth (Greece). Although, unlike the one at Ras il-Wardija, they are natural caves, these are equipped with rock-cut couches (each of the innermost caves even contains a cult niche) and were used as banqueting rooms for the communal feasts of a cult group dedicated to Melikertes / Palaimon and to Dionysos in the 5th and 4th centuries BC. The 'hall' set-up with couches for banqueting seems to highlight the interaction between ritual practice and architecture (Mylonopoulos 2006: 79-80; Nielsen 2014: 52(Fig. 30)-3; see also 232, 251). Remaining in Greece, in the sanctuary of Dionysos in Thorikos in the ancient Greek region of Attica, a room was cut into the rock and furnished with a 2.85 m broad bench. Dating to the 5th century BC, this room was rebuilt and divided into two in the 4th century BC (Nielsen 2014: 50(Fig. 29)-1, 232; see also 251). It may have also served as a banqueting hall/s.

Another possible banqueting hall from Pergamon in the region of Mysia in north-west Asia Minor (modern Turkey) could be identified on the terrace of the theatre by the podium temple of Dionysos. The whole structure was spread over three terraces and contained several rooms. Besides being decorated with red wall paintings and marble slabs on its floor, the main hall was equipped with couches / *klinai* and a cultic niche that was also clad with marble (Nielsen 2014: 53-4; see also 232, 251).

Though set in a building (not in a cave), the banqueting hall of the Dionysiac cowherds (*boukoloi*), also at Pergamon, provides another striking parallel, particularly to the presumed roofed structure added in extension to the cave. Including its different rebuilding and enlargement phases, this rectangular hall (at Pergamon) dates from the 2nd to the 4th century AD. Its association with Dionysos is strengthened by the presence of painting fragments in the hall which show Dionysian motifs while the many fragments of lamps that were found may indicate nocturnal rites. The interior of this Pergamon hall is divided into two facing banqueting rooms, each equipped with U-shaped benches or couches (*triclinia*). The doorway leading to both banqueting rooms lies in the middle of one of the hall's longer sides while, across from this doorway, there is a cult niche on the wall opposite the same doorway. Each of the banqueting benches consisted of a raised podium with a slightly lower shelf or ledge on the front to accommodate food and drink (Figure 26. See also Ascough, Harland and Kloppenborg 2012: 224(B6)-5(Fig. 21); Nielsen 2014: 118(Fig. 82)-20, 253, 261(Plate 21). For purposes of parallelism, see also Wenning and Gorgerat 2014: 7-8). A feature known also from mithraea, the front lower shelf or ledge confirmed that the main purpose of these two facing rooms was for communal meals. In this example, this feature seems to appear with the final rebuilding and enlargement of the said rooms during the late Roman period (second half of the 3rd century A.D.). It is missing from the banqueting set-up of the earlier phases of the same rooms / hall (Nielsen 2014: 118(Fig. 82)-20, 161). This internal set-up also seems to recall the one inside the cave at Ras il-Wardija – especially, its wall niches and rock-cut benches or couches with their front lower shelf or ledge

Figure 26. The banqueting hall of the Dionysiac cowherds (*boukoloi*) at Pergamon, in Asia Minor (modern Turkey). The interior of this hall was divided into two facing banqueting rooms, each equipped with U-shaped benches or couches. (Source: Ascough, Harland and Kloppenborg 2012: 225(Fig. 21)).

(Figures 20, 28) – but, in particular, the set-up of the presumed later external extension to the cave with the similar rock-cut benches / couches and front lower shelf and, not least, the U-shaped arrangement of the two newly-created facing spaces (Figures 24, 27).

Thus, evidently recalling the reclining couches seen in a *triclinium* or dining room set-up, the rock-cut U-shaped benches or couches at Ras il-Wardija may have also accommodated communal (ritual) feasts or banquets (Figure 29). As the latter (along with the presence of niches) were a common – yet not exclusive – feature of Dionysiac cults (see Nielsen 2014: 253; Nilsson 1985: 145-6), one may think of a possible cult of Dionysos, of his Punic counterpart Shadrapa, or of both of them in assimilation with each other among those cults practised at Ras il-Wardija. This possibility has already been considered

Figure 27. The rock-cut benches / couches running parallel to the cave's facade. The U-shaped arrangement of the two facing spaces may have formed an extension (inside a roofed structure) to the U-shaped arrangement inside the cave. The arrangement also looks very similar to that in the banqueting hall at Pergamon shown in Figure 26. (Source: *MISSIONE 1965*: Plate 89).

Figure 28. The cave interior with its U-shaped bench / couch arrangement and niches. (Photograph © NAG-National Archives Gozo).

Figure 29. A banqueting scene inside the cave. An artist's impression.
(Drawing: Joseph Calleja).

earlier in 2.4 above while discussing the presumed Dionysos Botrys face mask from Xlendi Bay. A possible assimilation of Dionysos with Shadrapa will be treated also in 3.9 below. But, even in the absence of any figurative representations, Dionysos (whether or not in assimilation with Shadrapa) might have also been worhsipped in aniconic form (see Gaifman 2012: 124, 223-5). A column donated to the *bakcheion* (a cultic hall of a Dionysian association) recorded in an inscription from Herakleia-Perinthos in Thrace (Nielsen 2014: 253) might have been, in fact, an aniconic representation of Dionysos.

Furthermore, one cannot fail to note how the 'banqueting' room / cave and its presumed later external extension on the fifth terrace might have impressively dominated the temple structure on the first terrace down below as happened, for example, at the sanctuary of Demeter and Kore on the Akrokorinth (at Corinth, Greece) (Mylonopoulos 2006: 80; Nielsen 2014: 46) to the extent that any communal feasts possibly undertaken inside the room / cave and its presumed later external extension might have surpassed other ritual activities. At the same time, while any rituals undertaken in the temple building on the first terrace may have secured communication with the divine (see 3.4 above), the presumed communal and ritualised feasting / banqueting in the fifth terrace's room / cave and its presumed later external extension may have played a communicative role amongst those partaking of the banquet. Simultaneously, it may have secured the participating group's sense of identity by creating a sense of unity amongst the participants and by defining the exclusiveness of the group in relation to other social groups (as in Azzopardi 2014: 151-2; Des Bouvrie 2012: 57, 61, 68; Iddeng 2012: 28-30; Mylonopoulos 2006: 70, 77, 79, 83-4; Prent 2003: 89). An on-site estimate revealed that the cave could have accommodated up to around fifteen reclined participants while its presumed later external extension could have provided an additional space for a maximum of around forty-five more reclined participants, bringing the total to a maximum of around sixty reclined participants occupying both cave and its presumed later external extension.

In summary, it seems that, dictated by the need for enlargement, the rock-cut screening wall of the cave was removed (see above) and rock-cut benches / couches were formed within an external roofed structure as an extension to the rock-cut reclining couches inside the existing cave and to which they look very analogous (Figure 24). In this manner, the newly-added dining space beyond the cave may have constituted two facing U-shaped banqueting rooms with reclining couches (the two parallel couches in the presumed banqueting room to the north may have constituted a *biclinium* in contrast to the U-shaped *triclinium* in the facing room, unless an in-built perpendicular extension on the sloping northern edge facilitated another U-shaped *triclinium* similar to the facing one) like the example of the Dionysiac cowherds at Pergamon (see above). As in the last example and like the rock-cut reclining couches inside our cave, these presumed rock-cut couches beyond the cave also had a lower front shelf or ledge, presumably to accommodate food and drink.

On the other hand, the smaller height of the presumed reclining couches outside the cave compared with that of those inside the cave may, perhaps, account for a hierarchical arrangement of the ritual banquet participants (as in Nielsen 2014: 206; see also 231, 235) with the most senior ones presumably occupying the space inside the cave. Likewise, the cave's apparent remains of a rock-cut screening wall (see above) may have been purposely left standing to mark a spatial division accounting for the same hierarchical arrangement. This presumed hierarchical arrangement may have, for instance, represented a distinction between two main initiation grades (as in Bremmer 2014: 95-6, 133; Nielsen 2014: 198-9 (including footnote 17), 200-2 (including footnote 36), 203-6, 224, 227(footnote 223), 251. See also below), perhaps implying a relatively small congregation (as in Bremmer 2014: 134) of no more than sixty participants (see above). Similar hierarchical arrangements could be noted, for example, in several mithraea where sections of former walls were sometimes left standing for the purpose of division in this respect whenever such mithraea (e.g. the *mitreo delle pareti dipinte* at Ostia) were enlarged (Nielsen 2014: 161, 163 (including Fig. 114); for similar arrangements, see 37 (including footnote 11), 203).

Then, a short passage extension running westwards perpendicular to the main passage in front of the cave (at Ras il-Wardija) may have provided the entry point to the presumed banqueting complex (Figure 24). This seems to be also suggested by what might have been a threshold on the westernmost end of this short extension (*MISSIONE 1964*: 171, Fig. 12, Plates 76-8; *1965*: 128, 135, Fig. 8, Plates 81, 86, 91(2), 100(2)). On the northern side of this presumed entry point, there were also three small rock-cut floor cavities any of which may have been somehow associated with some sort of a closing device for the presumed entrance (*MISSIONE 1964*: 171, Fig. 12, Plates 76-8), further suggesting an external (built) extension to the cave, which extension is expected to have been also roofed if it's entrance used to be shut.

No ceramics were found inside the cave (*MISSIONE 1964*: 172). However, the very few ceramic fragments found in the foundations of a posteriorly-built wall partially blocking the (present) entrance to the cave (*MISSIONE 1965*: 127) but particularly those few (including four tiny fragments of arretine ware) found in the (earlier disturbed) soil outside the cave, in the area of the presumed cave's extension, belonged to ceramic vessels that could have been associated with dining. These vessels included vases (including small ones), pitchers / jugs, and shallow bowls or plates / dishes (*MISSIONE 1964*: 172-3) and would seem to confirm the nature of the presumed cave's external extension – and, by implication, of the cave itself too – as a banqueting space.

What appears to have been another rock-cut offering table with two conical cavities was located at the point of intersection of the (presently) external passage in front of the cave's (present) entrance. This would have also been located next to the entrance of the presumed cave's external extension (Figure 24). Its location's significance will be discussed in 3.7 below. But subsequent need for more banqueting space inside the presumed cave's external extension may have necessitated the insertion of two perpendicular stone blocks along two of the offering table's edges (Figure 30) evidently to facilitate the extension of the 'bench' and 'pavement' (reclining couch) whilst hiding the offering table permanently from view (*MISSIONE 1964*: 171-2, Fig. 12, Plates 76-8; *1965*: 131, Fig. 8, Plates 86, 90(1)-1(2), 94(3), 100(2)). Fragments of plaster, to which a Roman date was assigned by the excavators, were found along the external length of the larger stone block (*MISSIONE 1964*: 172). This plaster may have survived from the Roman-period restoration suggested above. The basin resulting from the insertion of the two stone blocks yielded, from its infill, a ceramic sherd and a small stone column with a spiral rendering on its surface (*MISSIONE 1965*: 140, Fig. 8, Plates 86, 91(2), 94(3), 102(3)).

Figure 30. An extension to the 'bench' and 'pavement' at the passage's point of intersection in front of the cave. This was done by inserting two perpendicular stones along two edges of a rock-cut offering table. (Source: *MISSIONE 1965*: Plate 91(2)).

The deposition of the small stone column inside the resulting basin and above the offering table which the same basin came to integrate would seem to suggest a previous association of the column with the offering table to the extent that, when the latter went out of use, the column was deliberately deposited above it, forming (perhaps together with the single ceramic sherd found) a structured deposit. Both its apparent association with an offering table and its surface treatment would seem to indicate that this column was a betyl presumably receiving offerings on its associated offering table. Due to its sacred character, this column / betyl was not only maintained within the sacred precinct but was also deposited in close association with the offering table (as if to preserve the link) when the latter went out of use. This column / betyl is discussed at greater length in 3.8 below.

A fourth rock-cut offering table was found at the southernmost extent of the (presently) external passage (Figure 31). This offering table comprised two almost cylindrical cavities and had what could have been traces of a platform on its rear (*MISSIONE 1965*: 130-1, Fig. 8, Plates 88, 91(1), 100(1)). If, as suggested above, the (presently) external rock-cut 'pavements' and 'benches' formed an extension – presumably within a built and covered structure – to the rock-cut reclining couches inside the cave, this offering table might have stood in front of a niche (like those inside the cave) to which the platform belonged and within which a representation – aniconic or otherwise – of a deity might have received the offerings.

On a 'bench' on the southern side of and very close to the offering table, there was an engraving of an intriguing sign (Figure 31. *MISSIONE 1965*: 131,153-5, Fig. 8, Plates 88, 91(1), 94(1)) similar to which there is one engraved on a high rock outcrop at the Punic tophet of Sant' Antioco, in Sardegna (Figure 32. *MISSIONE 1965*: 153-4, Plate 108(3)). A similar sign was met with at Tas-Silġ sanctuary in Malta where it was found on a stone block and on dedicatory bowl fragments (*MISSIONE 1965*: 59, 154, Plates 38(2), 108(2)). The presence of this sign on offering bowls at Tas-Silġ sanctuary and its presence next to an offering table at Ras il-Wardija sanctuary would seem to put this sign in association with offerings (*MISSIONE 1965*: 154). A 'cross' sign was, then, to be seen engraved on another 'bench' a little farther away on the eastern side (*MISSIONE 1965*: 131, Plates 91(1)-2(1), 94(2)).

Further south, beyond the (presently) external passage but always on the fifth terrace, a large basin or pool with an internal flight of ten steps reaching down to its bottom, was cut (and, later, enlarged) perhaps for ritual bathing or immersion, possibly of initiates (Figures 24, 33). Measuring approximately

Figure 31. Offering table and an intriguing sign (enlarged inset). The offering table was situated at the southernmost extent of the passage outside the cave. The intriguing sign was engraved very close to it and may have been associated with offerings. (Source: *MISSIONE 1965*: Plates 91(1), 94(1)).

Figure 32. The sign at the Punic tophet of Sant' Antioco, in Sardegna. It is engraved on a high rock outcrop at the said tophet and is similar to the one from Ras il-Wardija shown in Figure 31. (Source: pierluigimontalbano.blogspot.com.mt/2015/04/archeologia-e-scrittura-i-triangoli.html. Accessed: 18-1-2017).

3.63 m by 3.24 m and having an average depth of 2.82 m, it could hold around 37.5 m³ of water (*MISSIONE 1965*: 136, 167, Fig. 8, Plates 76(1), 101(1); *1966*: 83-5, Fig. 12, Plates 58-9). Closer to the cave but beyond the (presently) external passage, there was a bell-shaped cistern with a rectangular opening and raised border (Figures 24, 34). In a second stage, it was widened and deepened (*MISSIONE 1965*: 133, 135-6, 167, Fig. 8, Plates 75-6(2), 97(2), 102(1); *1966*: 82-3, Fig. 11, Plates 56-7). Indicative of water storage, the use of cisterns in a religious context implies the use of and reliance on water much needed both for purification and as a constituent of ritual (as in Guettel Cole 1994: 207. See also Nielsen 2014: 67, 73, 75, 77, 83). Therefore, this cistern is likely to have stored water either to supply any rituals taking place inside the cave and in its presumed external extension (as in Lauter 1979: 441-2 cited in Nielsen 2014: 73(footnote 147)) or to supply the basin or pool. The ritual function suggested by the site's excavators immediately above for the basin or pool may be due to the latter's location before one reaches the heart of the sacred area on the fifth terrace. This may also indicate that the point of access to the site was through the fifth terrace.

Thus, upon entering the sanctuary, one would ritually cleanse or purify himself / herself by means of ablution rites performed in the basin / pool before proceeding into the sanctuary. This would be much the same like the application, upon one's entry into a church, of holy water on his / her forehead from holy water stoups purposely located by churches' doors. But the basin / pool could have been also associated with initiation rites involving cleansing (as in Apuleius, *The Golden Ass* 11. 48. 23; Bowden 2010: 133; Bremmer 2014: 5; Demosthenes, *On the Crown* 259-60 (quoted in Nielsen 2014: 225); Nielsen 2014: 4, 213, 227, 236) for

Figure 33. The rock-cut basin or pool on the fifth terrace. (Source: *MISSIONE 1966*: Plate 58(2)).

which purpose, it would also be expected to be located by the sanctuary's entrance much like baptism fonts (when they were still located next to the churches' main entrances) for the administration of baptism: a Christian initiation rite (Nielsen 2014: 182, 186, 207, 229. See also Bowden 2010: 45, 209-10) involving the cleansing of sins. Pools like the one at Ras il-Wardija, in fact, are frequently found located

Figure 34. The rock-cut water cistern on the fifth terrace. (Photo: The author).

next to the respective sanctuary entrance in association with rites of passage / initiation or purification rites (as in Bremmer 2014: 94, 104, 119-20, 157; Nielsen 2014: 58) and, presumably, not least with possible rites of initiation into Dionysiac mysteries (see 3.9 below). Following the ritual cleansing, the initiates could have moved in procession (perhaps, involving also ritual dancing) (as in Bremmer 2014: 5-8, 83, 89, 98, 104; Nielsen 2014: 204-5 (including footnote 63), 207, 209, 212, 215) to the cave and presumed built extension on the same terrace where, reclining on the rock-cut couches, they might have engaged themselves in a communal banquet (as in Bremmer 2014: 105; Nielsen 2014: 4-5; see also 197-9, 202, 213-4) perhaps as part of a Dionysiac mystery cult (see 3.9 below).

Choruses of singers and dancers were current in rural Dionysiac festivals (Kerényi 1976: 321). If the enactment of this proposed ritual performance – procession / dancing – at Ras il-Wardija took place in the open air, it would have had the benefit of reinforcing the dramatic effect of the same performance (as in Prent 2003: 87). At the same time, any 'tiered' arrangement of spectators on the multi-levelled slopes of the site (see 1.1, 3.2 above) may have enhanced the spectators' observation and visual experience of the ritual performance (the procession / dancing). Likewise, it may have also enhanced the communicative potential of the procession / dancing. Tiered arrangements for spectators – even if on a larger scale than the one suggested for the Ras il-Wardija sanctuary – are especially (but not exclusively) frequent in sanctuaries of Dionysos and of Demeter and Kore like those in Corinth, in Lykosoura, in Pergamon (Mylonopoulos 2006: 94-7), and in Eleusis (Nielsen 2014: 201).

The basin / pool also yielded eleven small stone troughs from its muddy infill (Figure 35. *MISSIONE 1966*: 85-6, Plate 60). Other small stone troughs included those found in the soil covering both fourth and fifth terraces (*MISSIONE 1965*: 140, Plate 102(4-5)) and two very small ones that were found among the stones of the presumed ramp (*MISSIONE 1967*: 92) providing access to the sanctuary (see 3.2 above). In a religious context, these small portable stone basins might have served as small portable offering tables (*mensae sacrae*) in connection with votive offerings. Similar examples – albeit used in association with offerings to the dead – are known from the Fazzān region in Libya where they occur in different types, not least in types like ours (Mattingly & Edwards 2003: 199(Fig. 6.22a), 210-2 (including Figs. 6.33-4), 222(Fig. 6.40a); Mattingly (ed.) 2007: 8 (including Fig. 0.7), 95-8 (including Figs. 9.6, 9.8-10, 9.15, 9.18), 109-14 (including Figs. 10.19, 10.21-8), 184-8 (including Figs. 18.4, 18.8-9, 18.16, 18.19)). Seventeen such basins (from Ras il-

Figure 35. Stone trough found in the rock-cut basin or pool. It was one of eleven small stone troughs retrieved from the muddy infill of the said basin or pool and which are now kept in storage at the Gozo Museum of Archaeology. (Photo: The author).

Wardija) are still preserved in the reserve collection of the Gozo Museum of Archaeology. As these – and particularly those found deposited in the basin / pool – were all found within the sanctuary's space, they might have been deposited there as part of the sanctuary's ritual closure when both sanctuary and pool went out of use; at the same time, keeping them within the same sacred precinct and preventing their re-use (as in Glinister 2000: 56-60, 67-70).

But as significant accumulations of objects (especially if concentrated in small areas) in votive or ritual contexts might indicate production rather than religious activity (Gleba 2009: 78, 81) and as suggested by signs of stone extraction (some of which may have represented a later activity) on the first, third, fourth, and fifth terraces (Figure 25. *MISSIONE 1965*: 133-7, 145-7, Plates 76(2), 97-100, 104-5(1, 3), 106-7(1); *1966*: 88-90, 133, Plates 61(2)-2), these small stone basins might have also been surviving products of a workshop associated with the sanctuary. Sanctuary workshops, in fact, are known from elsewhere in the Mediterranean world and in Europe too (Brody 1998: 55-6; Ghey 2007: 27; Gleba 2009: 76-81; Nakhai 2001: 147), possibly, including also Tas-Silġ sanctuary in Malta (Azzopardi 2014: 117). In this case, the stone for the basins would have been extracted from the sanctuary site itself whilst, sourcing stone from a sacred place like a sanctuary, might have also contributed towards the sacred character of the basins.

The ceramic content obtained from the fifth terrace was largely of a third to second-century BC date along with other specimens of no later date than the 1st century AD (*MISSIONE 1965*: 138, 142) as was that from the neighbouring fourth terrace (*MISSIONE 1965*: 138, 142, Fig. 10(1)). Of these, few plates' and cups' fragments were found in a rock cavity on the fifth terrace towards the fourth while an almost half of a small Roman cup of reddish clay was elevated from the rock landslides between the fifth and fourth terraces (*MISSIONE 1965*: 139). The substantial size of the latter along with its apparent isolation but mostly the findspot of the former fragments may suggest that they formed a structured deposit, having possibly been intentionally deposited as part of a ritual termination of an associated cult or ritual closure of the sanctuary itself (as in Glinister 2000: 69-70).

3.7 Sacrality of doors: doorways with offering holes or other sacred features

The close association the offering holes enjoyed with the entrance's threshold of the enclosure / *temenos* wall that surrounded the temple structure on the first terrace (see above) and a similar association of two other sets of two offering holes respectively with the original (and present) entrance to the man-made cave on the fifth terrace and with the entrance of the presumed cave's external extension on the same terrace (see below) might have borne a similar significance. All three instances might also recall similar situations in the earlier (Maltese) prehistoric temples where similar holes sometimes appear in association with doorways.

In antiquity, portals or doorways often enjoyed an aura of sanctity. Being a medium of entrance and exit, the doorway could have been a material expression of what in religious belief was perceived as a 'bridge' linking this natural world of earthly beings with the supernatural world of spirits and deities (see Azzopardi 2014: 56). These two worlds would have been aptly and respectively represented by the 'world' outside a temple and the 'world' inside the temple but both linked by the temple's doorway.

But like betylic pillars (that, as sacred stones in which deities dwelt, were objects of worship), doorways could also mark the very dwelling places of the deities themselves and, thus, could also serve as their material images. In Mycenae (in Greece), for instance, the sanctity of portals or doorways was highlighted through their associations with cult objects like altars (as two sacral erections: altar and doorway) but, more frequently, with sacred trees or with cult symbols. Three Mycenean gold signet rings show portal shrines in association with sacred trees. A gold-plated silver ring (also Mycenean) shows a holy gateway supporting a cult object in the form of a pair of horns of consecration as a sign of the gateway's sanctity. Finally, a steatite bead seal from a Mycenean beehive tomb at Ligortino in Crete shows a gateway in association with a sacred tree, a horned cult object and a crescent symbol connected to a lunar deity (Evans 1901: 181-5). Evidently to highlight its sanctity, the so-called 'Lions' Gate' at Mycenae also carries a betylic pillar (substituting a sacred tree) between two guardian lions on top of its lintel.

Associations of doorways with cult objects to highlight the former's sacred character were also observed by the fifth-century BC Greek historian Thucydides at Athens. In his *History of the Peloponnesian War* (6. 18. 27), Thucydides noted that, in Athens, it was common to find stone herms (semi-figural representations of deities) in the doorways of both private houses and temples (Gaifman 2012: 67). Pillars or non-figural monuments generally associated with Apollo Agyieus / Apollo of the Streets were also often set up at the porch of or entrance to Dorian houses, sometimes to ward off evil (Gaifman 2012: 123-5, 272-3, 277; see also 283, 287). In his *Description of Greece* (4. 33. 3), the second-century AD Greek geographer and traveller Pausanias also noted a herm associated with a gate in Messene, in ancient Greece. This herm was, in fact, set at the Arkadian gate that led to Megalopolis (Gaifman 2012: 66, 69). To highlight their sanctity, gates were also sometimes named after deities (including minor deities). One such example is provided again by Pausanias (*Description of Greece* 1. 44. 2) who noted a gate called 'the Gate of the Nymphs' in the old gymnasium in Megara, also in ancient Greece (Gaifman 2012: 70).

The religious significance and sanctity attributed to gateways is also alluded to by the Babylonian priest and historian Berosus who flourished in the 3rd century BC. Quoted by Flavius Josephus in his *Against Apion* (1. 19. 140), Berosus speaks of gateways' decoration (in Babylon) in conformity with their sanctity. The biblical book of Psalms also appears to assign preferential treatment towards gates or doors on account of their religious significance when these are exhorted to provide access to the King of glory / the Lord God (Psalm 24(23): 7, 9), when manifesting the Lord's affection towards the gates of Zion (Psalm 87(86): 2), and when gates are associated with righteousness (and the righteous) and with the Lord God Himself (Psalm 118(117): 19-20). Then, in the biblical gospel of John (10: 9), the gate is given a divine character as Christ calls Himself the gate that guarantees salvation to those entering through it / Him.

As the god who embodied the threshold, Hermes was the god of the metaphorical threshold, signifying, for example, the threshold of adulthood (Gaifman 2012: 154). Hekate was worshipped by the Greeks as a goddess of entryways, particularly in Caria, in Asia Minor, while a triple image of the same goddess as Hekate Epipyrgidia was set up by Alkamenes in the 5th century BC at the entrance to the Athenian acropolis (Gaifman 2012: 167 (including footnote 122)). And, finally, one cannot fail to mention that, to highlight the divine character of doorways, the Romans also had a specific god of the door. This god was named Janus and was represented as double-faced in personification of the entrance and exit elements of the door (see above).

Therefore, one should not be surprised that, to emphasise the sacred character of the entrance's threshold of the enclosure / *temenos* wall surrounding the temple structure on the first terrace at Ras il-Wardija, a ritual feature – in this case, an offering table – was incorporated in such a close association with it (Figure 17). The inclusion of two similar ritual features (i.e. offering tables) respectively on the southern side of the original (and present) entrance to the man-made cave on the fifth terrace (Figure 20) and on the southern side of the entrance to the presumed cave's external extension (Figure 24) might have borne a similar significance being likewise associated with an entrance. The former ritual feature (i.e. the one by the cave's entrance) also consisted of two conical cavities where offerings might have been presented in front of an idol – whether it was figural or aniconic – placed on what looks like a small rock-cut platform on the cavities' rear (*MISSIONE 1965*: 128-9, Fig. 8, Plates 79-80). The latter (i.e. the one by the entrance to the presumed cave's external extension) consisted of two similarly conical cavities where offerings might have been presented in front of a column-shaped betyl placed on the cavities' rear (see 3.6 above, 3.8 below). The presence of an idol in both instances would have also further highlighted the sacred character of the respective entrances they were associated with.

As it may have known no temporal or geographical boundaries, it seems logical to think that this tradition of emphasising the sacred character of doorways by associating ritual features with them might have been either in continuation of an earlier tradition or formed part of a set of distinct but similar traditions. Thus, one may perhaps safely assume that similar ritual features sometimes encountered in doorways of Maltese prehistoric temples like Skorba and Ġgantija northern and southern temples (Evans 1971: 36, 175, 177, Plans 9, 38A, Plates 3(6), 28(4-6), 29(1)) are likely to have served the same purpose.

Unless it was meant as an apotropaic device to keep away any external malign 'intruders' in the form of evil spirits or other similar supernatural agents (see Gordon 2015: 76-81), a structured deposit beneath a threshold at Ġgantija (in Gozo) might have borne a similar significance. This structured deposit (possibly, serving also as a foundation deposit) consisted of an inverted bowl containing 158 sea-shells along with a bovine's horn and potsherds and was found during excavations in 1933 beneath the main entrance's threshold leading into the southern prehistoric temple at Ġgantija (Evans 1971: 173, Plan 38A, Plate 25(3-4)). This deposition could have also served to emphasise the sacred character of the threshold / doorway in question, especially through the inclusion in it of a bovine's horn. A bovine was a rather elite sacrificial animal and bovine images (presumably, even their corporeal remains like horns) might even be memorials of sacrifice (Akar Tanriver 2015: 129). Derived from the actual horns of the sacrificial bovines, the use of the so-called 'Horns of Consecration' as ritual elements in Minoan and Mycenaean religious contexts also underscores such horns' sacred character. Alternatively, as bovine horns constituted the original drinking vessels (the precursors of the rhyton / artificial drinking horn) (Kerényi 1976: 60), the broken tip with a tiny perforation on our bovine horn (currently, on permanent display at the Ġgantija Visistors' Centre) from Ġgantija may suggest a primitive drinking vessel perhaps used in drinking rituals and, thus, of a sacred character. Even in such a case, its deposition under a threshold would have borne the same significance in highlighting the sacred character of the threshold / doorway in question.

Through its apparent association with another prehistoric temple's doorway, a stone relief discovered at Tas-Silġ sanctuary in Malta may have borne a similar significance. Showing a standing female figure typical of those usually identified as fertility divinities, this stone relief was found very close to the prehistoric temple's entrance (*MISSIONE 1964*: 75-6, 191, Fig. 4f, Plate 30; *1968*: 118) whose sacrality it may have, thus, underscored.

In a funerary context, then, a doorway could have likewise enjoyed a sacred character but with a somewhat different significance. Being again a medium of entrance and exit (see above), the doorway could have been a material expression of what in religious belief was perceived as a bridge linking this world of the living with the world of the dead respectively respresented by the 'world' outside the burial chamber (or complex) and the 'world' inside.

It may have thus been in view of the above that ritual and funerary features also seem to highlight the sacrality of the threshold at the entrance to the prehistoric Xagħra Brochtorff Circle underground burial complex. On one side of and in association with the Tarxien phase (3150-2500 BC) threshold stood what was probably a carefully-built shrine or altar, possibly mirrored by a similar structure on the opposite end. However, the entrance's sacrality may have been further enhanced by the presence of cut features across the entrance. These features could have been pits containing deliberate depositions that consisted of pottery, chert and obsidian fragments, whilst one of these cut features contained a figurine fragment. In addition to these, a burial pit located by the northern edge of the same threshold may have helped to accentuate even further the sacrality of the burial complex's entrance with the deceased's bones that the same pit contained (Stoddart *et al.* 2009: 111-8 (including Figs. 8.3-9)).

Yet the same Xagħra Brochtorff Circle yielded what might have been another example of an entrance's highlighted sacrality. A small plain stone betyl (usually referred to as a 'statue menhir') with crude engravings of the basic human facial features on its top part making it look like a primitive version of the Classical semi-figural herm was found in the entrance of the west chamber of a Żebbuġ phase (4100-3700 BC) double-chambered tomb (Malone, Bonanno *et al.* 2009: 222, 282, Fig. 10.46; Malone, Stoddart *et al.* 2009: 100). Besides having possibly been meant as an apotropaic device providing protection to the deceased buried inside, the presence of the betyl in the entrance of the burial chamber may have also highlighted the sacrality of the same chamber's entrance.

Having said all this, it seems that the phenomenon of associating ritual objects or features with entrances or doorways to highlight the latter's sacred nature was not restricted to Classical antiquity when the Ras il-Wardija sanctuary was in use. At least in the Maltese scenario, it seems that this phenomenon can be detected already in earlier prehistoric times.

3.8 Stone worship

One important find which the excavators came across while excavating the temple on the first terrace was that which they called a 'cippus'. This stone 'cippus' (Figure 36) was found in the space between the external wall of the quadrangular temple structure and the presumed shallow enclosure or *temenos* wall surrounding the said temple structure. It was also near the temple's entrance and the offering table outside but in front of the said entrance (Figure 37. *MISSIONE 1966*: 104, Plate 75(3-4). See also above). This stone 'cippus' assumes the shape of a pyramid standing on a base or a pedestal as if to highlight the pyramid's significance. Presently kept in storage at the Gozo Archaeology Museum, it also carries faint traces of thin creamy white plaster with which its surfaces are likely to have been originally covered.

Figure 36. Stone pyramidal 'cippus' or betyl. Assuming the shape of a pyramid, it stands on a base or pedestal as if to highlight the pyramid's significance. It is kept in storage at the Gozo Museum of Archaeology. (Photo: The author).

Taking into account not only the location where it was found but also its treatment (i.e. plastered surfaces and pedestal support), the stone 'cippus' is very likely to have been a betyl. Stone betyls were often perceived – typically in Levantine and Aegean traditions – as the abode of the deity (or where the deity's power resides) or the deity's own aniconic representation (Budin 2014: 206-7; Crooks 2013: 5-6, 8; De Vincenzo 2013: 261, 265; Evans 1901: 112-3, 132-3). Symbols or inscriptions on or near betyls stating the latter's identification with named gods confirm this (see examples in Gaifman 2012: 212, 215-7, 220, 309; Wenning 2001: 80-4). Thus, betyls were considered as animated stones possessing divine or magical (sometimes, even demonic) power and were often believed to have fallen from the heavens, like the meteorites that were especially venerated as sacred stones in the Roman East (Gaifman 2012: 20, 24, 56, 74, 116-7, 308; Wenning 2001: 80). As a result, animated stones could also be iconographically anthropomorphised, generally with the addition of facial features, no matter how rudimentary they might be (see examples in Wenning 2001: 83-5, Fig. 3. See also Gaifman 2012: 308-9). In this respect, such stones may be also considered as schematised 'statues'. With their primitive and rudimentary appearance, these (and other betyls) may sometimes be also viewed as the antecedents, first of the so-called (semi-figural) herms (Gaifman 2012: 36, 234-8, 305-6) and, then, of the artistically more developed figurative cult images (Gaifman 2012: 232-4, 305, 311-2). As they shared the same nature of cult statues, betyls were, like these, hosted inside temples (De Vincenzo 2013: 261). Such stones, therefore, not only enjoyed pride of place in cultic places but were themselves the object of worship: the so-called 'litholatry' (worship of stones).

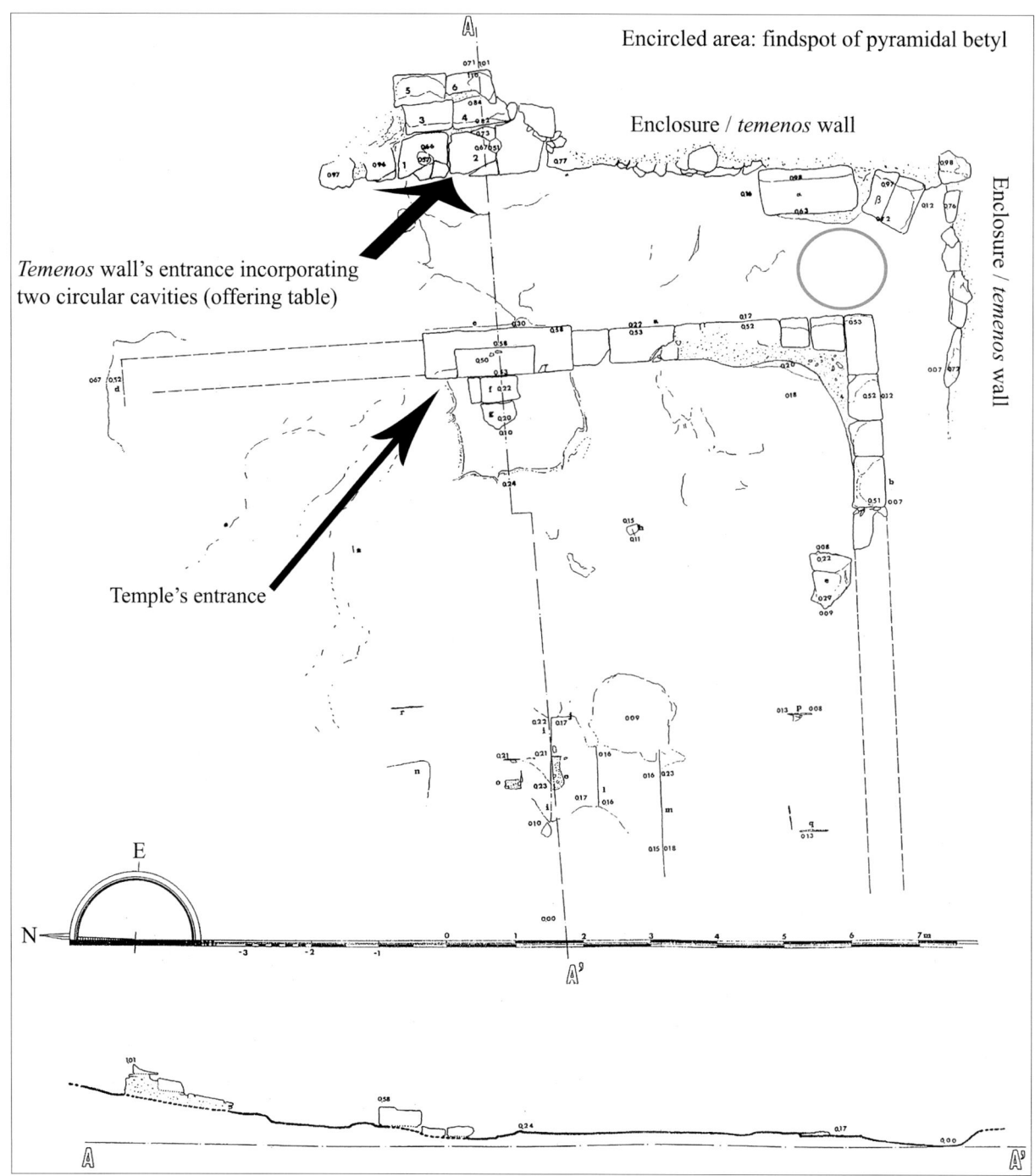

Figure 37. Plan of the temple on the first terrace showing the findspot (encircled) of the pyramidal 'cippus' or betyl. The latter was found between the external wall of the temple and the presumed *temenos* wall, near the temple's entrance and the offering table in front of the said entrance. (After *MISSIONE 1966*: Fig. 13).

Though often lacking any iconographic elements or accompanying inscriptions, such stones served ritual functions. They can be so identified from the context – usually, a religious context – in which they are to be found, from the conspicuous location or position they usually enjoy, and / or from the treatment (like ornamentation) they sometimes receive. These qualifying elements – namely, religious context, conspicuous location / position, and treatment – are shared by both betyls and statues, rendering them equivalent to each other.

These stones may assume different sizes and shapes. Small ones might have been intended to be portable (see Wenning 2001: 81). Especially when worked, their shapes usually range from pillar-like to spherical, conical or ovoid but other shapes different than these are also sometimes encountered. In certain instances, however, and particularly in prehistoric contexts, they may retain their natural shape. Many are found fixed in the ground while others may be freestanding but they are almost always in conspicuous locations or positions. They may come from both urban and rural (or extra-urban) settings, could be also (though not quite frequently) decorated or carry some iconographic elements, and may occur singly or in pairs (Crooks 2013: 1, 8).

Perhaps less frequent are those betyls assuming a pyramidal shape. One such stone comes from a temple site at Nora (in Sardegna) while two others come from Tharros (also in Sardegna), respectively from the so-called 'archaic temple' on Capo San Marco and from the necropolis. These three pyramidal stones are about 30 cm high; almost of the same height as the one from Ras il-Wardija. The example from the Tharros necropolis consists of a pyramid on top of a small square pillar carrying a Punic funerary inscription. While certain scholars do more readily claim these pyramidal betyls to have represented the Carthaginian goddess Tanit (Figure 38), Sabatino Moscati adopts a more cautious approach (Moscati 2005: 151-2, 186-7, Figs. 17, 39; Pesce 2000: 219-21, Fig. 85. For the example from the small fifth-century BC sanctuary at Capo San Marco, see also Brody 1998: 59-60 (including note 121), Figs. 60-1). In fact, pyramidal stones are known to have represented other deities too. In his *Description of Greece*, the second-century AD Greek geographer and traveler Pausanias noted a small pyramidal stone representing Apollo Carinus in the old gymnasium near 'the Gate of the Nymphs' in Megara (1. 44. 2) and another pyramid representing Zeus Meilichius in Sicyon (2. 9. 6), both in ancient Greece. Pyramidal stones of Aphrodite are also known from the Orient (Gaifman 2012: 67(footnote 67)). Another pyramidal betyl (Figure 39) was recently found in the southern necropolis at Tharros (now on permanent display at the Archaeological Museum of Cabras, Sardegna) while more are turning up in excavations conducted by Anna Chiara Fariselli and Carla Del Vais in the same necropolis (Anna Chiara Fariselli personal communication). In funerary contexts, betyls (including pyramidal ones like these) may have served as memorial marks for the dead, perhaps equivalent to the Nabataean '*nephesh*' (Wenning 2001: 80. See also Budin 2014: 206-7). But, also on account of their association with the funerary sphere, they might have been even perceived as the abode of the spirits of the dead (or their aniconic representation), unless they represented deities protecting the buried deceased.

Nonetheless, a dedication of the small temple on the Ras il-Wardija coastal promontory to Tanit might have not been out of place at all either. In its heyday, the temple structure on the first terrace must have not only dominated the coastal promontory but must

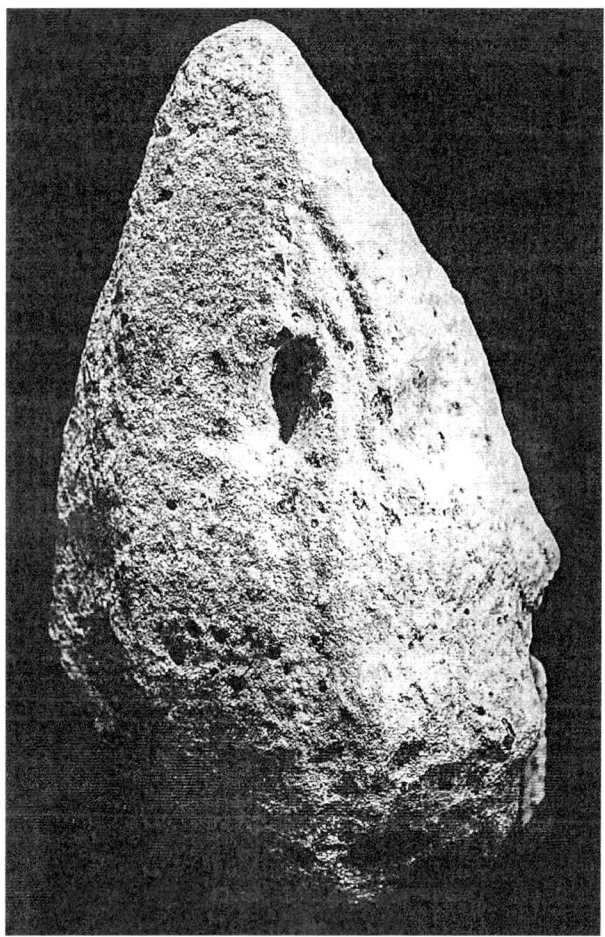

Figure 38. Pyramidal betyl claimed to represent Tanit. It was found in the small 'archaic temple' on Capo San Marco, Sardegna. (Source: Pesce 2000: 220(Fig. 85)).

Figure 39. Pyramidal betyl from the southern necropolis at Tharros, Sardegna. It is on display at the Archaeological Museum of Cabras, Sardegna. (Photo: The author).

have also borne a certain significance to sailors to whom it must have been visible when navigating along this coastal stretch or approaching either the nearby harbour of Xlendi or the sheltered anchorage at Dwejra.

Significantly, Tanit was a marine deity invoked by mariners. The sign of Tanit is sometimes portrayed on a Carthaginian coin and funerary stelae in association with dolphins. Dolphins were important for ancient sailors as their presence around ships was believed to indicate an impending storm or change in sea conditions (Brody 1998: 32, Figs. 11, 14-15, 20). Tanit's protection of sailors and ships is also illustrated by further maritime attributes in association with her sign. Her sign is sometimes depicted in association with ships (or parts of ships, like the prow or stern) or even mounted on standards placed on board ships (Figure 10. Brody 1998: 32-3, Figs. 16, 18-19). On other occasions and particularly on stelae, Tanit's sign accompanies nautical symbols like anchors which may symbolise the goddess's protection of sailors from storms or steering rudders which may attest to the goddess's importance for the safe navigation and guidance of ships (Brody 1998: 33, Figs. 17, 20, 67a). Like her Phoenician predecessor and equivalent goddess Astarte, Tanit was a celestial deity and, thus, shared with her celestial attributes like the solar disc and crescent moon. These celestial symbols, in fact, make their appearance in relation to the sign of Tanit on Carthaginian sacrificial stelae (Brody 1998: 32, Figs. 13, 15). Presumably representing the same goddess, the solar and lunar symbols appear in association with ships (where these symbols sometimes appear mounted on poles), again suggesting the goddess's protection of sailors and ships (Brody 1998: Figs. 66, 67b).

The Carthaginian Tanit is also known to have been worshipped at the harbour sanctuary of Tas-Silġ in Malta (*MISSIONE 1963*: 89-91, 95-6, 151, Fig. 15(1-6), Plates 29(2-4)-30(1-7)) and, thus, cannot be excluded to have been worshipped in Gozo too where her Phoenician predecessor Astarte is already evidenced (*CIS*, I, 132). In view of the above, the Ras il-Wardija coastal promontory is expected to have provided an ideal location for her cult.

Levelled-out rock floor found almost in the middle of the quadrangular temple structure on the first terrace at Ras il-Wardija could have accommodated the plinth (*MISSIONE 1966*: 97-8, Fig. 13, Plate 70(1-2); *1967*: 90, Fig. 9, Plate 40(2)) on which the discovered betyl might have stood inside the said temple structure during the latter's heyday. This might have been around the 3rd century BC which does not only mark the earliest use of the site (see above) but, in a wider Mediterranean context, also witnessed an envisioning of the primeval past marked by the adoption of non-figural monuments for veneration (Gaifman 2012: 88, 108). As the betyl inside faced the temple's entrance, offerings could be made on the offering table facing it outside (Figure 40. See also above). The scene might have been typical of imageless shrines befitting the description – imaginary, yet related to reality – provided by Apollonius Rhodius in his *The Argonautica* (2. 1169-76) with respect to the shrine of Ares by the southern shores of the Black Sea where the Amazons practiced stone worship and sacrificed to the stone on an altar that, like the offering table at Ras il-Wardija, faced the stone from outside the temple (Gaifman 2012: 110-2; see also 305).

When the temple structure (or the betyl itself) at Ras il-Wardija went out of use, the betyl appears to have been removed from its central place but was maintained within the sacred precinct and close to the offering table perhaps on account of its sacred character (as in Glinister 2000: 56-60, 67-70). The discovery of what appears to have been a struck coin (undecipherable) and part of a small metal chain in the same area where the betyl was found (*MISSIONE 1966*: 107) may suggest that, along with the betyl, these may have formed a structured deposit perhaps marking the termination of the ritual use of the betyl or even of the temple itself (as in Glinister 2000: 69-70). A similar chain fragment made of gold was found at Tas-Silġ sanctuary in Malta (*MISSIONE 1965*: 37, Plate 24(4)).

Another possible betyl might have been a stone in the shape of a small column of a height ranging from 23 cm to 25.5 cm. Its surface looks to be rendered in the form of a spiral (Figure 41. *MISSIONE 1965*: 140, Plate 102(3)). What appeared to the present writer to be possible tiny characters scratched in a vertical orientation on the column's surface when this is in an upright position did not convince the Phoenician epigraphist Maria Giulia Amadasi Guzzo. On examining digital images of these features, she could not detect

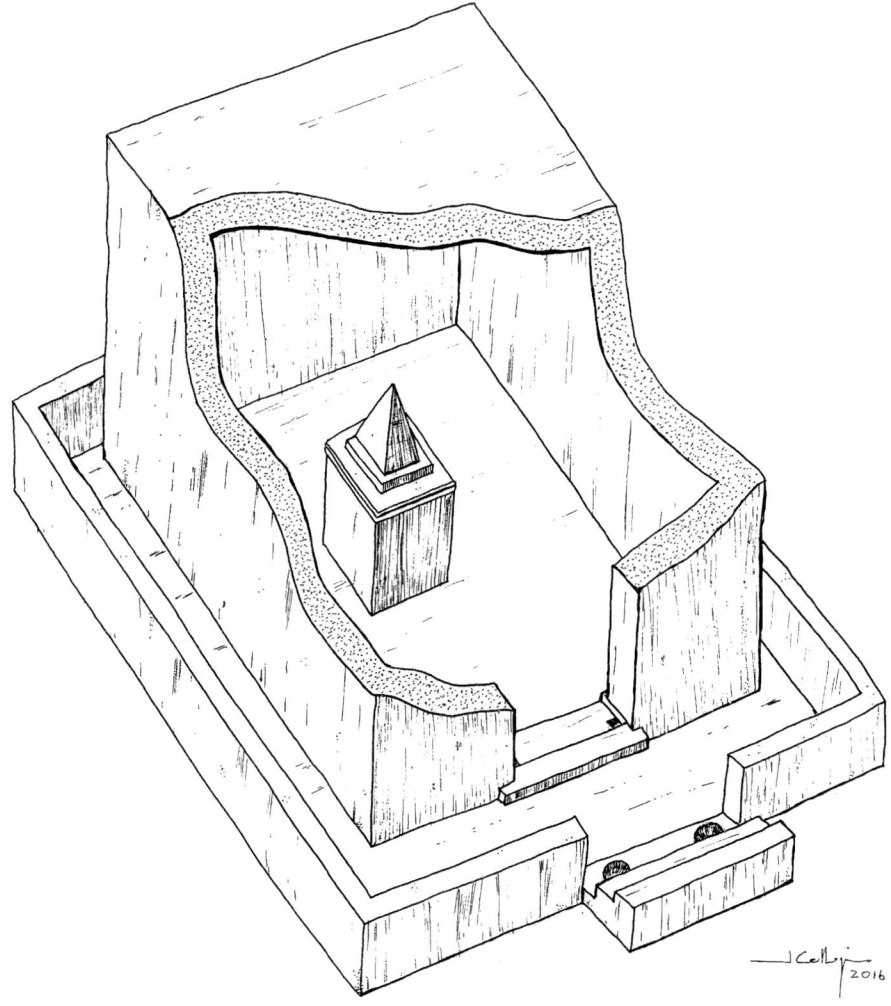

Figure 40. The pyramidal betyl as it might have looked inside the temple on the first terrace. An artist's impression with a cut-out view showing the interior. The betyl might have stood on a plinth, facing the temple's entrance and the offering table beyond from where it could have received offerings. (Drawing: Joseph Calleja).

Figure 41. A small stone 'column' betyl with a spiral rendering. It was found deposited above the offering table and within the basin created with the insertion of two stones around the same offering table at the passage intersection in front of the cave. It is now kept in storage at the Gozo Museum of Archaeology. (Photo: The author).

any legible text or single letter (Maria Giulia Amadasi Guzzo personal communication). But the stone's betylic nature seems to be suggested not only by its surface treatment (i.e. its spiral form) but also by the context in which it was found.

As shown in 3.6 above, a set of two rock-cut conical cavities following an arrangement very similar to that of the two offering tables also mentioned above were found beyond and in front of the (present) entrance to the cave on the fifth terrace. They lay at the intersection of the (presently) external passage which they seem to have found themselves forming part of. It appears that this offering table had to make way for an extension of the 'bench' and 'pavement' (reclining couch) relative to the above-mentioned passage intersection (Figures 24, 30). Consequently, the offering table went out of use when two stone blocks of different sizes were inserted to create a continuous 'bench' / couch on the side of the same passage, at

the same time creating what the excavators termed 'a basin' with the two conical cavities consequently finding themselves on its bottom (Figure 42). The infill within this basin and above the two conical cavities yielded the above-mentioned small stone column that seems to have been deliberately deposited above the two conical cavities with which it might have been previously closely associated. In fact, along with a ceramic sherd found within the same infill, the small stone column may have formed a structured deposit marking the termination of the ritual use of both presumed offering table and associated stone column.

This would seem, therefore, to confirm that the pair of two conical cavities comprised an offering table behind which might have stood the stone column as a betyl or an

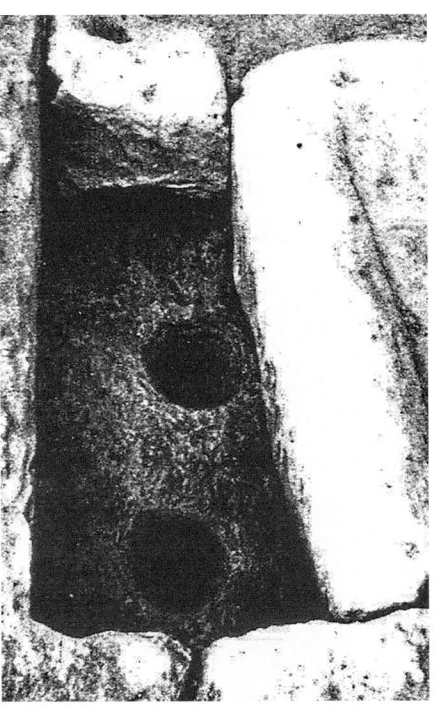

Figure 42. The offering table at the bottom of the basin at the passage intersection in front of the cave. The basin was created with the insertion of two stones around the exposed edges of the offering table. The small stone column came from the infill within this basin and above the offering table. (Source: *MISSIONE 1965*: Plate 94(3)).

Figure 43. The standing 'column' betyl overlooking the offering table. An artist's impression showing the 'column' betyl in relation to the offering table with which it was found associated and, thus, from where it could have received offerings. (Drawing: Joseph Calleja).

aniconic representation of a deity to whom offerings were made on the offering table (Figure 43). When both offering table and stone column / betyl went out of use and their ritual use was terminated, the stone column / betyl was deposited over the offering table and everything was covered over, both to maintain the sacred objects within the sacred precinct (as in Glinister 2000: 56-60, 67-70) and to enable the continuation of the rock-cut 'bench' / couch flanking the passage way.

It is unclear whether the presumed structured deposition of both pyramidal betyl and 'column' betyl marked the termination of the sanctuary's use (in the case of the pyramidal betyl's deposition) or solely the termination (or replacement) of the aniconic cults themselves. But as no figurines or figurine fragments are reported to have been found at the Ras il-Wardija sanctuary complex (including the temple structure on the first terrace), it may be suggested that the cult at Ras il-Wardija remained largely aniconic throughout. Very schematic figures are engraved on the interior of the man-made cave on the fifth terrace. One such deeply-engraved cruciform figure on the internal wall of one of the niches of the said cave (Figure 21. See also 3.6 above) is sometimes claimed to be a representation of Tanit. But although this cruciform figure is semi-anthropomorphic like the common schematic symbol of Tanit consisting of a triangle or a betyl with outstretched arms and head, it lacks any secure attributes of this goddess while it could have also been made in later times of the sanctuary's lifetime (see 3.9 below). A discussion of these figures will follow in the forthcoming section.

3.9 Possible mysteries and the enigmatic cruciform and 'flying' figures

As shown in 3.6 above, engraved 'flying' and cruciform figures make their appearance on the interior of the man-made cave on the fifth terrace. These figures are very schematic and lack any attributes to aid their identification. As a result, they have always baffled researchers in their attempt to understand their nature and decipher their meaning. In an attempt to provide an interpretation, alternative possibilities will be proposed as, each in its own right, may look plausible. Thus, this attempt does not pretend to solve definitely the questions surrounding the identification and meaning of these figures but rather seeks to address them in their local and wider contexts, aware of the limitations posed by the scanty evidence available.

Stone worship has already been discussed in 3.8 above where this phenomenon was witnessed in the guise of worshipped betyls. The cruciform figures, in particular, could have, indeed, marked a development stage in the course of this phenomenon. Schematic cruciform figures that are very similar to the cruciform ones at Ras il-Wardija appear on a stela from the Punic tophet at Nora, in Sardegna (Figure 44) and on another stela from the Punic tophet at Sulcis (Sant' Antioco), also in Sardegna (Figure 45). These cruciform figures are interpreted by Sabatino Moscati (2005: 212(Fig. 62)-3, 218(Fig. 69)-9) as possibly representing a transitional stage in the evolution from aniconism to iconism (or anthropomorphism) in the form of a betyl which is humanised with the addition of two outstretched arms (see also Pesce 2000: 196). The schematic cruciform figures from Ras il-Wardija may, perhaps, be also thought of as being an imitation of cruciform herms (Figure 46) which, in their semi-figural form (see Gaifman 2012: 36, 234-8.

Figure 44. Schematic cruciform figure in relief from Nora (modern Pula), Sardegna. It appears on a stela from Nora's Punic tophet. (Source: Moscati 2005: 212(Fig. 62)).

Figure 45. Schematic cruciform figure in relief from Sulcis (Sant' Antioco), Sardegna. It appears on a stela from Sulcis' Punic tophet. (Source: Moscati 2005: 218(Fig. 69)).

Figure 46. A cruciform herm of the god Hermes. This herm is to be found at the Museo Nazionale Romano Palazzo Massimo, Rome. (Photo: The author).

Also 3.8 above), may likewise represent a transitional stage in the evolution from aniconism to iconism (see Gaifman 2012: 232-4. Also 3.8 above). If the schematic cruciform figures at Ras il-Wardija are also assumed to represent such a transitional stage (without, however, excluding alternative explanations), it may, therefore, be suggested that these semi-anthropomorphic figures post-date the pyramidal betyl and, presumably, also the small temple on the first terrace that accommodated it as well as the small 'column' betyl found in front of the cave on the mentioned fifth terrace. They might have been carved, in fact, in a later stage of their hosting cave's lifetime.

Presumably reflecting this transitional stage, the schematic cruciform figures at Ras il-Wardija may also be possibly linked with a cult of Dionysos – or, perhaps, with mysteries incorporated into a cult of Dionysos – whom, thus, they could have represented in semi-figural form and who, as seen earlier (see 2.4, 3.6 above), may have been one of the deities worshipped at Ras il-Wardija. As it exerted widespread religious influence, the cult of Dionysos enjoyed a universal character generally embodying and sometimes even dominating over other gods while surpassing geographical boundaries. This enabled his cult to naturally develop into a cosmopolitan religion, particularly in later antiquity (Kerényi 1976: 387-8. See also Nielsen 2014: 207).

An important development in the history of ancient religion comprises the emergence of the so-called 'mysteries' or 'mystery cults' with most of them (including those of Dionysos) flourishing in the Hellenistic and Roman periods (Bianchi 1976: 4, 13, 15; Bowden 2010: 139, 203, 211; Nielsen 2014), sometimes even in sanctuaries dedicated to Syrian and Phoenician deities in both eastern and western Mediterranean (Nielsen 2014: 93-106, 124, 140(Fig. 99)-52, 242-5, 252-3). They often survived till late Roman times (Bowden 2010: 147, 198-9, 204, 206-7, 208-10, 213; Nielsen 2014) like the Dionysian ones taking place on Mount Parnassos (in central Greece and overlooking Delphi) as recorded in c. 400 AD by Macrobius in his *Saturnalia* (1. 18. 5, also quoted in Kerényi 1976: 237 (including footnote 154)). They could be also celebrated in places outside sanctuaries proper, like wealthy private residences or the private halls of groups of initiates (Nielsen 2014: 107-19, 125, 132-3, 135, 160, 207, 231-7, 250, 252-3; Nilsson 1985: 145-6).

The early Archaic period of the Greek world was marked by contacts with the Near Eastern and Egyptian cultures. For this reason, it is also aptly known as the 'Orientalising period'. During this period, Oriental cults inspired Greek mysteries to which they introduced eschatological ideas and beliefs in life after death. Later, in Hellenistic times, Greek mysteries (particularly the Eleusinian mysteries) inspired the creation of mysteries in the Oriental religions (Nielsen 2014: 198; see also 218-9, 226).

Amongst the several mysteries or mystery cults, one would find the so-called 'Orphic' initiations and mysteries closely connected to the Dionysian cult. Widely spread in Sicily and south Italy, the central doctrine or tradition of Orphism was that of the suffering and dying Dionysos Zagreos based on the myth wherein the young Dionysos is betrayed, slain, butchered / dismembered, and eaten by the Titans and, then, reanimated by Demeter (Bianchi 1976: 1; Bremmer 2014: 57-8, 62, 72-7, 79-80, 105, 108; Clement of Alexandria, *Exhortation to the Greeks* 2. 17. 2-18. 2; Kerényi 1976: 231, 242-3, 245-6, 249, 267, 271, 373; *LIMC* III/1: 541; Morford and Lenardon 1999: 246 cited in Edmonds III 2013: 100-1; Nielsen 2014: 25, 212-6(footnote 137); Nilsson 1985: 12, 40-1, 121, 138-9; Nonnus, *Dionysiaca* 6. 169). In Dionysian religion, Dionysos' sacrifice and cruel death was enacted in the form of a sacrificed animal / young bull (Kerényi 1976: 179-80, 189-93, 236, 245, 247-8, 250, 269; see also 321-4) following which the god descended into the underworld from where he was to return afterwards (Kerényi 1976: 181-4, 192-3, 248, 294). In a way, the Dionysiac myth also reflects the slaying of Orpheus himself by the Thracian women who, according to the Augustan mythographer Conon, tore him to pieces after a performance of secret rites (Bremmer 2014: 57; Kerényi 1976: 267; Nielsen 2014: 27).

In his *Dionysiaca* (6. 155. See also Kerényi 1976: 114, 245), Nonnus narrates how Persephone gave birth to (Dionysos) Zagreos, 'the horned infant'. The epithet 'Zagreos' would qualify Dionysos as hunter or capturer of living animals (see below) but, at the same time, his horns would identify him with the hunted / sacrificed horned bull. On the small island of Tenedos off Troy, a young bull wearing hunting boots befitting a little (Dionysos) Zagreos was, then, sacrificed to Dionysos. In other words, Dionysos is both hunter and hunted / victim (Kerényi 1976: 114-5, 190, 270, 321, 329, 333, 379-81; see also 173 where, in Athens, a special sacrificial bull was singled out with words usually used to invoke Dionysos). This seems to recall the Cretan feast of Dionysos held every second year and during which a whole bull was torn to pieces. In this great Dionysian sacrifice, the sacrificial animal (the bull) represented a suffering, dismembered god. The fate of the bull child / horned infant born to Persephone was no different from that of the sacrificial animal / bull (Kerényi 1976: 115-6; see also 203) with whom he (i.e. Dionysos) was identified (Kerényi 1976: 182, 203, 236). This fate appears to be also indicated in a scene on a Roman sarcophagus of *c.* 190 AD (see below).

Often celebrated in symposia-like gatherings usually taking place in 'triclinium' set-ups, the abovementioned mysteries included the consumption of food and particularly of meat (Euripides, *Cretans* fr. 472.9-19, quoted in Bremmer 2014: 66. See also Burkert 2012: 44; Iddeng 2012: 23; Nielsen 2014: 207, 209, 213-4; Nilsson 1985: 135; Rasmus Brandt 2012: 153-5) which, in the case of the celebrated Dionysiac theme of the suffering and dying Dionysos Zagreos, would have reflected or represented the slaying or sacrificing of Dionysos and the 'consumption' of his body by those taking part in the gathering for their own well-being (for the origins of this notion, see Kerényi 1976: 86-7. But see also Obbink 1993: 65ff). The main functionaries in these mysteries were often sacral 'cowherds' (*boukoloi*) (Kerényi 1976: 351-3; Nielsen 2014: 120 (including note 42), 209) or, perhaps, their 'priest' equivalents in different regions (see Nielsen 2014: 210). In certain cases, priestly duties in public cults could also be performed by initiates as priests or lay priests (Nielsen 2014: 207). Mysteries associated with Dionysos / Bacchus were prevalent in the western Mediterranean, though not so commonly in connection with public cult (Nielsen 2014: 95, 125, 210. See also Bremmer 2014: 148; Kerényi 1976: 237). Nonetheless, geographically and contentwise, Dionysian mysteries (like other mysteries) were highly variable throughout the long duration of their existence (Bremmer 2014: 78, 100-1; Nielsen 2014: 208, 210, 212, 241; Nilsson 1985: 144. See also Bowden 2010: 130, 165).

The communal meals would follow initiation rites (as in Apuleius, *The Golden Ass* 11. 48. 24. See also Bowden 2010: 166; Nielsen 2014: 4-5, 197, 206, 209, 213-4, 221, 224, 227, 231. Also 3.6 above) that developed out of and drew upon patterns of seasonality and life-death-revival cycles. These rites were usually performed by fundamentally agrarian societies and, as death and revival was often a core feature of such initiations, dying deities like the slain Dionysos Zagreos (see above) provided a model for the mysteries and initiation into them (Nielsen 2014: 1, 5, 14). Initiation rituals, in fact, were frequently performed in connection with myths of dying (and reviving) gods symbolising the agrarian year and were celebrated at great festivals. One of these gods was Osiris, whose myth of death (and revival by Isis) used to be celebrated by the Egyptians near his many tombs that were to be found around Egypt and continued unchanging into the Hellenistic and Roman periods in parallel with new Hellenised mysteries (Nielsen 2014: 10-11; see also 215, 220 (including footnote 169)). Osiris was assimilated with Dionysos according to Diodorus Siculus (*Library of History* 1. 11. 3, 4. 1. 6), Herodotus (*The Histories* 2. 42. 2, 144. 2), and Plutarch (*On Isis and Osiris* 13, 35). So much so, that the myth of Dionysos Zagreos (see above) may have even been modeled on the old Egyptian myth of Osiris (Edmonds III 2013: 348; Nielsen 2014: 215(footnote 130), 219. See also Bremmer 2014: 111; Nilsson 1985: 40). Also according to Herodotus (see citation immediately above), Osiris / Dionysos was one of the chief deities of the underworld on account of his association with the death and resurrection cycle of the seed, of the Nile waters, and of the moon phases (Vella 1993: 216. See also Champeaux 2002: 146-7; Nilsson 1985: 66). The Egyptians commemorated the death (including dismemberment) and resurrection of Osiris symbolised by the sowing and sprouting of corn after the retreat of the flood waters while the return of the waters symbolised the re-birth of Osiris. In its turn, the re-birth / resurrection of Osiris symbolised eternal life renewed and promised immortality (Vella 1993: 218-9). A sculpture in the sanctuary of Magna Mater in Ostia (near Rome) showing the god Attis dying under a pine tree includes also a smaller representation (of the same god) that may symbolise his revival. This seems to further suggest initiations and mysteries that were practised at this Ostian sanctuary at least till the end of the 4th century AD (Nielsen 2014: 91). Rites of this sort are unlikely to have been completely alien amongst the essentially agrarian populations of both Gozo and Malta.

Caves or grottos (including artificial ones) were especially associated with Dionysiac cults (Bremmer 2014: 103; Nielsen 2014: 250-1, 253; Nilsson 1985: 61-2. See also Bowden 2010: 121). But, symbolising the underworld and initiation into death, the dark atmosphere often provided by a crypt or a cave would have also been an ideal setting for initiation rites (Nielsen 2014: 4, 18, 33, 70, 123, 215-6, 221; see also 250-1). In fact, grottos often form part of sanctuaries with initiations and mysteries (Bremmer 2014: 103; Nielsen 2014: 73, 114, 125, 200-1, 214, 250-3. See also Porphyrius, *On the Cave of the Nymphs* 6-7 quoted in Nielsen 2014: 153(footnote 180)) where they (i.e. the grottos) might have played the role of *telesteria* / initiatory shrines where mysteries could be held (see Bianchi 1976: 13). The ensuing banquet would have required special installations like *klinai* / reclining couches and a shrine or shrines (Nielsen 2014: 4, 47-8(footnote 53); Nilsson 1985: 63, 145. See also Nielsen 2014: 100, 109, 214, 221, 231). Both features seem to be present in the rock-cut cave at Ras il-Wardija where the reclining couches are cut in the rock and the similarly rock-cut niches in the walls may have served as shrines (Figure 28). The rock-cut 'pavements' and 'benches' beyond the cave also seem to have been reclining couches (see 3.6 above). Reclining while eating was a Near Eastern tradition imported into the Greek world during the Orientalising period (Nielsen 2014: 206(footnote 80)).

However, communal meals need not have been always part of mystery celebrations. At times, they could also be part of assemblies of cultic groups or religious associations, whether or not their members were initiated in mysteries. Thus, dining halls (including cave-like rooms) could be used for the celebration of mysteries as well as for religious assemblies (Nielsen 2014: 5, 13, 25-169, 196, 214, 217-8, 231-2, 252-3; Nilsson 1985: 62-4); sometimes even for initiations if there was no other place where these could be performed (Nielsen 2014: 61, 124-5, 214, 252).

Apart from mystery groups, religious associations dedicated to Dionysos are known too (Bremmer 2014: 100; Nielsen 2014: 112-25, 232). Private or secret 'wild parties' celebrating Dionysos might also take place, particularly at night and in the countryside. During such parties, not only wine was consumed but also sexual indulgence or orgies might have taken place (Bowden 2010: 105; Jameson 1993: 60; Kerényi 1976: 237-8, 240-1, 328. See also Nielsen 2014: 215(footnote 129), 219). Regarded as the Old Dionysos, the Phrygian god Sabazios was also celebrated in a similar manner in Athens and Pompeii (Nielsen 2014: 139, 141, 225 (including footnote 211)-6; see also 251).

On a side-note, one may perhaps recall the local folk tradition about members of a secret sect frequenting the cave at Ras il-Wardija (*MISSIONE 1965*: 126) which may possibly have its origins rooted in the above-presumed ritual activities. This tradition may, in fact, constitute a transmission – in a manner typical of traditions – of a forgotten memory concerning ritual feasting activities that presumably have once taken place there perhaps, at times, even discreetly. A similar folk tradition / memory involving ghost women and the playing of cymbals also survived until the beginning of the 20th century in the vicinity of Mount Parnassos (in central Greece and overlooking Delphi) on which Dionysian festivals are known to have been still celebrated until *c.* 400 AD (Kerényi 1976: 237. See also above).

Mysteries of Dionysos were very popular, particularly during the Hellenistic and Roman periods, and were often performed in special-purpose rooms (Nielsen 2014: 2, 114(Fig. 79)-24, 208-18, 247, 251. See also Bowden 2010: 133). They may have also formed part of a non-Greek Dionysian religion in the Semitic world which, nonetheless, was not introduced there from the Graeco-Roman world but borrowed late Graeco-Roman art and architectural forms (Kerényi 1976: 256-7). At Petra (in Jordan), in some of the public sanctuaries dedicated to Dushara (often identified with Dionysos) and / or to al-Uzza (sometimes identified with Aphrodite) and dating mostly to the 1st century BC-1st century AD, dining (and assembly) set-ups were cut in the rock (Nielsen 2014: 97, 140(Fig. 99)-2, 250, 252; Wenning and Gorgerat 2014: 1-11) similar to what evidently happened also at Ras il-Wardija. Sacred banquets seem to have been celebrated also in honour of the Kabeiroi – who, like Dionysos, were also gods of wine – in a hall evidently equipped purposely with benches at the mystery sanctuary of the Kabeiroi at Chloe on the Greek island of Lemnos in the Aegean Sea and in an extra-urban sanctuary outside Thebes in ancient Greece (Nielsen 2014: 22(Fig. 10)-4, 205). Evidently associated with a sanctuary, the presumed mysteries celebrated in the room / cave and in its presumed external extension at Ras il-Wardija would seem to have been either collective mysteries or mysteries bound to a public cult (see Nielsen 2014: 2, 30, 46-50, 197, 252), while the use of the room / cave and its presumed external extension by specific religious groups or cultic associations cannot be excluded either (as in Nielsen 2014: 5, 13, 25-169, 196, 233-6, 241, 246, 248, 252-3). Cults of Phoenician deities did not include mysteries (Nielsen 2014: 3, 9, 102) in pre-Hellenistic times (Nielsen 2014: 93; see also 198), although they could include religious associations (Nielsen 2014: 3, 9, 233-5, 252). But in Hellenistic times, a possible assimilation of the Phoenician / Punic Shadrapa with his Greek equivalent Dionysos under prevailing Hellenistic influences cannot be excluded and, thus, celebration of the mysteries of Dionysos in assimilation with Shadrapa may be deemed equally possible. Certain Roman provinces (like Africa and Pannonia) did, in fact, witness assimilation of Dionysos with indigenous gods (Nilsson 1985: 131). Similarly, syncretistic mixtures of local and foreign cults (including mysteries) are also known from late Roman Italy (Nielsen 2014: 124).

Evidently in keeping with the notion of the suffering god (who, then, triumphs over suffering) (Kerényi 1976: 70-1), the theme of the suffering / dying Dionysos Zagreos was also represented iconographically. Depictions of Dionysos / Bacchus Zagreos about to be slain may show him with outstretched hands in a manner not dissimilar to the cruciform (and 'flying') images carved in the cave / 'triclinium' at Ras il-Wardija. One of the best known depictions of this theme is the one shown on an ivory pyxis now kept in the Museo Civico Archeologico in Bologna, Italy. This pyxis was fashioned not earlier than the 5th century AD but was made after an ancient original and recalls the Orphic myth. One of the Dionysiac scenes on this pyxis shows a newly-born Dionysos seated on an initiation throne in the cave (where he is born) and with his hands outstretched. He is in the process of being lured before he is slain (Figure 47. Kerényi 1976: 265, Plate 66B; Kerényi 1980: 253; *LIMC* III/1: 559(265, 267); III/2: 455(265), 456(267)).

Figure 47. A Dionysiac scene shown on a late antique ivory pyxis. The scene shows the newly-born Dionysos Zagreos on an initiation throne and with outstretched hands. He is in the process of being lured before he is slain. The pyxis is in the Museo Civico Archeologico in Bologna, Italy. (Source: *LIMC* III/2: 456(267)).

With further reference to the suffering / dying Dionysos, a cruciform structure is shown on an Attic chous in the Metropolitan Museum of Art in New York. Consisting of a long pole and a crossbeam, this cruciform structure is carried by a group of children in a marriage procession of Dionysos in Athens (Figure 48). Evidently a vestige of the Dionysian idol, this structure would appear again much later in representations of the myth of Dionysos' childhood (Kerényi 1976: 305, 308-9, Plate 93). In fact, this cruciform structure appears also on a Roman sarcophagus of *c.* 190 AD in the Walters Art Museum, Baltimore, Maryland (USA). The central scene on this marble sarcophagus depicts the Triumph of Dionysos but one of the scenes forming a frieze on the lid of the same sarcophagus shows an aged silenus approaching the child Dionysos to whom he brings the cruciform structure that was carried in procession in Athens (see immediately above) as an allusion to his pending fate (i.e. his slaying) and subsequent stay in the underworld (Figure 49. Kerényi 1976: 378, Plate 137). The iconography of this cruciform structure may, perhaps, also recall that of the cruciform herms (see above). For example, a triple cruciform herm from Tor Marancia (in Rome) but, now, in the Vatican Museum represents three sets of deities one of which is Bacchus / Dionysos shown in assimilation with the gods Apollo and Axiokersos on one of the herm's three cruciform sides (Figure 50. *LIMC* III/1: 559(261); III/2: 455(261)).

A figure described as 'lord of the wild beasts' appears on a Minoan gem from Kydonia, now at the Ashmolean Museum, Oxford. On this gem, the figure – highly probable to be a respresentation of the Cretan Dionysos – is shown with outstretched hands evidently resting on the respective heads of two flanking lions (Figure 51). As 'Oriental Dionysos', this type of figure was taken from the Near East into Hellenistic art to be later provided with wings (Kerényi 1976: 81, Plate 25). Very likely to be depicting Dionysos Zagreos, i.e. Dionysos as hunter or, rather, capturer of living animals (as the epithet 'Zagreos' would seem to imply)

Figure 48. A cruciform structure carried in a marriage procession of Dionysos in Athens. The procession scene is shown on an Attic chous in the Metropolitan Museum of Art in New York. (Source: Kerényi 1976: Plate 93).

Figure 49. An aged silenus approaching the child Dionysos with the cruciform structure (arrowed). This was the same cruciform structure carried in procession in Athens. The scene of the aged silenus with the cruciform structure appears on the lid of a Roman sarcophagus of *c.* 190 AD in the Walters Art Museum, Baltimore, Maryland (USA). (Source: https://www.bing.com/images. Accessed: 21-1-2017).

Figure 51. A probable representation of the Cretan Dionysos on a Minoan gem from Kydonia. Described as 'lord of the wild beasts', the figure on the gem is shown with outstretched hands evidently resting on the respective heads of two flanking lions. The gem is at the Ashmolean Museum, Oxford. (Source: Kerényi 1976: Plate 25).

Figure 50. Bacchus / Dionysos on a triple cruciform herm. He is shown in assimilation with Apollo and Axiokersos on one of the three cruciform sides of the herm that represents three sets of deities. The triple cruciform herm comes from Tor Marancia in Rome but is, now, in the Vatican Museum. (Source: *LIMC* III/2: 455(261)).

(Kerényi 1976: 81-4, 86-9), the Kydonian figure provides an unmistakably very close parallel to the cruciform figures – albeit without any flanking lions or other animals – respectively in niche / shrine 5 and on the left side of this same niche / shrine in the cave at Ras il-Wardija. All figures – the Kydonian one and the two Ras il-Wardija ones – might be imitating a common prototype but, as no animals show up in association with the latter, what might be represented here (at Ras il-Wardija) is another Dionysos but with a different attribute/s. What appears to be a rising pole above the cruciform figure's head in niche / shrine 5 at Ras il-Wardija (Figure 52) may perhaps recall the poles on which Dionysos' masks along with garments used to be set up in a semi-figural manner (Figure 9. See also 2.4 above) not unlike this very schematic and semi-iconic cruciform figure itself.

In the same cave, a schematic figure in 'flying' attitude is located between niches 1 and 2 and a possibly similar one on the left side of niche 5 where it is shown with a smaller cruciform figure on top (Figures 22, 23. See also 3.6 above). As an indication of the surpassing of the limits of nature, wings sometimes qualify the figures whom they characterise as divine (Kerényi 1976: 81). Unless they also represented the god Dionysos himself, these winged figures could have, therefore, represented chthonic or subterranean gods in association with Dionysos, himself also a subterranean god. Alternatively, these figures could have represented winged souls of the dead amongst whom Dionysos had dwelt in the underworld (see Bianchi 1976: 8; Kerényi 1976: 303, 311) or, perhaps, winged Erotes who accompanied and guided the deceased to the underworld (see Kerényi 1976: 365-9, 372-3, Plates 118, 121, 125, 130A, 131A). Possibly to highlight the significance of the underworld in initiations, these figures could have also represented winged female death daemons whose role might have been re-enacted by initiates. Often shown fleeing away, these Etruscan-style daemons also form part of Dionysian iconography (see Nielsen 2014: 216; see also 211(Fig. 132, middle register); Nilsson 1985: 125-6, 128-9). They may have also represented an incarnation of death (as in Nielsen 2014: 216(footnote 134)). But even if what may appear to be wings are, in fact, the figures' hands raised to the sky, these figures could have also represented a deity or deities. In this case, the represented deity or deities could have formed part of the myth on which the initiations and mysteries (presumably celebrated at Ras il-Wardija) were based (as in Nielsen 2014: 204).

While the 'flying' and cruciform figures respectively carved on the walls between niches / shrines 1 and 2 and on the left side of niche / shrine 5 in the Ras il-Wardija cave may have been left as votive graffiti by worshippers or visitors to the cave, the cruciform one centrally carved on the internal back wall of niche / shrine 5 might have been itself an object of worship and could have received offerings on a shelf inserted beneath (Figure 53). The remaining niches / shrines may have hosted similar figures. These were either engraved figures on the niches / shrines' internal back wall but are now completely eroded and no longer visible or, else, were free-standing three-dimensional representations resting on the same shelf where they received the offerings. But besides receiving worship, these presumed figures /

Figure 52. The cruciform figure in niche / shrine 5 inside the cave. What appears to be a rising pole above the cruciform figure's head may perhaps recall the poles on which Dionysos' masks used to be set up in the manner shown in Figure 9. (Source: *MISSIONE 1965*: Plate 83(3)).

representations could have also symbolised the god/s' presence or even his / her partaking of the sacred meal (as in Nielsen 2014: 9, 91, 125, 232, 241, 252. See also Kerényi 1976: 203). Alternatively, the remaining niches may have simply held (on their shelves, perhaps serving as altars) votive gifts (as in Nielsen 2014: 84) or service and cult implements used in connection with the ritual banquets (as in Nielsen 2014: 109).

Finally, initiates into mysteries (not only those of Dionysos) or those taking part in them (i.e. in mysteries) were generally promised a better life in this world (sometimes, they were even promised life after death), a higher order of morality or piety and, not least, safety at sea and protection against troubles, dangers, and storms (Nielsen 2014: 203-4; see also 214-5, 221, 225, 229 (including footnote 231)-30). Therefore, not only the temple building close to the edge of the cliff on the first terrace but also the complex (i.e. cave and its presumed external extension) presumably associated with mysteries and initiations on the fifth terrace might have been associated with the sea. In view of this, both first terrace temple building and fifth terrace complex may have been created by a maritime community whose needs they may have also addressed. This maritime community could have frequented the nearby Xlendi harbour or, perhaps, even the smaller yet sheltered and closer cove at Dwejra.

But participation in mysteries (including communal meals) could also be attested in early Christianity (Bremmer 2014: 162-3; Kerényi 1976: 258; Nielsen 2014: 2, 182, 236-7, 253. See also Bowden 2010: 209). In his *Exhortation to the Greeks* (12. 118-20, cited in Nielsen 2014: 229(footnote 233)), Clement of Alexandria

Figure 53. The cruciform figure with offerings in niche / shrine 5 inside the cave. As it might have been itself an object of worship, the cruciform figure could have received offerings on a shelf inserted beneath as shown in this artist's impression. (Drawing: Joseph Calleja).

refers to Christianity as the true mysteries in contrast with the Bacchic (Dionysiac) false mysteries. These Christian mysteries seem to have been somehow preserved to this day in the celebration of the mass which starts with an initiation rite asking for the forgiveness of sins followed by the celebration of the mystery of the Eucharist that ends with the distribution and consumption of the same Eucharist. In the mystery of the Eucharist and in an evident similarity with pagan mysteries (Nielsen 2014: 224, 229 (including footnote 233)-30. See also Bowden 2010: 45, 208-10; Bremmer 2014: 156, 160, 162-4), Christians celebrated (and still do) the death and revival / resurrection which the divine Christ went through like the gods referred to above.

It has already been shown above that mystery cults in both eastern and western Mediterranean often survived till late Roman times. The sanctuary at Ras il-Wardija may have also remained in use till late Roman times (see 1.1, 3.2, 3.5 above). At the same time, the Christianisation process on the Maltese islands was already under way in the late Roman period as suggested by palaeo-christian catacombs found at Rabat and in other places in Malta (Bonanno (with Cilia) 2005: 324-37) and by a North-African red-ware lamp of the 4th-6th centuries AD whose decoration includes the Christian 'chi-rho' monogram alongside the biblical theme of the two Hebrews carrying a huge bunch of grapes from the valley of Escol in Canaan (Numbers 13, 23) discovered at It-Tokk (today's Independence Square) in Victoria, Gozo (*MAR* 1961: 5, Plate V). This same biblical theme is also shown on at least three other lamps of the same type and period from Malta whilst another lamp (of the same type and period) whose 'dove' decoration may have been inspired by the (Christian) belief in deliverance from death (or resurrection) was also found in an open-air floor tomb of the *fossa* type in a quarry at Ta' Sannat, in Gozo (Azzopardi 2007: 33(note 56)).

Had the Christianisation process on the island of Gozo already begun while the room / cave and its presumed external extension at Ras il-Wardija were still in use in association with the presumed Dionysiac activities, one cannot exclude that, during the early stages of Christianisation, mysteries and symposia-like banquets celebrating the suffering / dying Dionysos Zagreos could have been assimilated to Eucharistic celebrations of the suffering / crucified / dying Christ by a religious group of people who were familiar with these Dionysiac celebrations and yet were experiencing a gradual transition to the new Christian phenomenon. Were these first-generation 'hybrid Christians' the last to use the room / cave and its presumed external extension for their Dionysiac-Christian celebrations? If yes, the engraved figures in the cave at Ras il-Wardija might have equally represented for them the crucified Dionysos Zagreos and the crucified Christ in assimilation with each other.

Participation in pagan mysteries or in the Christian mystery of the Eucharist required initiation which, in the case of Christians, is achieved through baptism: a Christian initiation rite (Bowden 2010: 45). If it is assumed that syncretised mysteries / celebrations were performed at this time at Ras il-Wardija, a similarly syncretised initiation rite / baptism might have also taken place there at this same time. This syncretised initiation rite / baptism might have also been performed in the open air, making use of the existing pool outside the cave and its presumed external extension (see Nielsen 2014: 229).

Such presumed scenario would have provided the setting where the two religious systems that seem to have been compatible and translatable among the two different religious groups could encourage mutual exchange and contact and push forward modes of interaction between the same two religious groups. Religious ideas and values could, thus, be shared through a multi-directional process of borrowing, accommodation, and restructuring, creating a middle ground wherein the two religious groups could co-exist, integrate, and interact and, ultimately, create a new hybrid religious identity (as in Demetriou 2012: 5-7; Nielsen 2014: 229 (including footnote 231)). Effectively, this may have paved the way for the eventual but gradual Christianisation of the presumed local Dionysiac cults through an elaborate process of syncretism. In all likelihood, this process would have been not only complex but also selective whereby previous elements might have been retained (possibly even reworked or reorganised) and new ones adopted or appropriated in response to new needs and aspirations. In other words, the process would have been marked by an ability to absorb new religious systems or cults into existing structures. This would also seem to confirm that, until it took a more distinctively Christian look in a progressive manner, local Christianity might have been rather of a hybrid character stemming from religious pluralism then still prevalent (see Azzopardi 2014: 307-8).

On the other hand, the same figures in the cave at Ras il-Wardija might have represented solely the crucified Christ had they been made in later times. Several Mediaeval graffiti of crosses and cruciform figures can be seen on the walls of the towers flanking the gate of the *Tour* of Domme (Dordogne, France). These graffiti were evidently left by Templar knights who were imprisoned there following their suppression. Some of the cruciform figures may reflect an attempt by the imprisoned knights (who engraved them) to assimilate themselves with the crucified Christ or to make allusion to the 'passion' that they and their order were subjected to (Curzi 2012: 129-30, 146(Fig. 20)-7(Fig. 21)). Some of these Mediaeval cruciform graffiti (Figure 54) bear a striking resemblance to the ones at Ras il-Wardija as does a low-relief carving of a crucifix on the south exterior wall of the late Mediaeval church of Santa Marija ta' Bir Miftuħ, limits of Gudja in Malta (Vella 2013: 159(Fig. 148)). Moreover, though found near the temple on the first terrace, a Mediaeval bronze coin probably of the Aragonese period may also attest to some sort of activity during this period at Ras il-Wardija (*MISSIONE 1966*: 107, Plate 76(4)). These combined occurrences would seem to indicate that a Mediaeval date for the engraved figures (at Ras il-Wardija) cannot be excluded either, perhaps in the context of rural monasticism for which the secluded Ras il-Wardija cave would have been an ideal location.

Figure 54. A Mediaeval graffito of a cruciform figure at the *Tour* of Domme (Dordogne, France). It was engraved on one of the walls of the towers flanking the gate of the *Tour* of Domme evidently by one of the Templar knights imprisoned there. (Source: Curzi 2012: 147(Fig. 21)).

A final alternative explanation would be that of an original depiction the meaning and significance of which are renewed and reinterpreted in later times by different people who, nonetheless, are accustomed to similar imagery (Bradley 2002: 115-6, 118, 123). In the case of the engraved figures at Ras il-Wardija, what could have been original semi-figural (or semi-anthropomorphic) depictions of the suffering Dionysos Zagreos might have been 'transformed' and given a new interpretation by Christians who, in later antiquity or in Mediaeval times, perceived in them a crucified Christ. This kind of religious behaviour could have also entailed a transformation of a Punic-Roman sanctuary into a Christian shrine or hermitage (as in Bradley 2002: 122-3; Brakke 2015; Chaniotis 2015; Emmel, Gotter and Hahn 2015; Frankfurter 2015: 149-55; Sami 2010: 220, 225-8, 230-3; Saradi 2015) as happened to the two cave-mithraea in Doliche (in Asia Minor) when these were reused by Christians who, in this case, themselves engraved crosses into some of the mithraic reliefs probably in the 4th century AD (Nielsen 2014: 156).

3.10 Regulating relations through ritual

One of the main roles of ritual is that of regulating relations between humans and divine beings (Morgan 1994: 107-8). Already the marginal location of the sanctuary, on a high and liminal place evidently 'unpolluted' from any habitations or settlements in its immediate surroundings, might have secured the ritual cleanliness often demanded of sacred spaces (as in Guettel Cole 1994: 216; Prent 2003: 87). On the other hand, the mobilisation of the associated community or communities for ritual activities in the sanctuary may have served to increase the cohesion of the social groups (of which the community or communities was / were composed) or, equally, the social power of certain individuals or groups through the common activities which the rituals may have involved (as in Jost 1994: 229).

Ritual sacrifices or offerings taking place in the temple on the first terrace may have been perceived as a pathway to make contact with the divine. On the other hand, the communal meals that may have taken place inside the cave and in its presumed external extension on the fifth terrace may have reached a communicative climax as they intensified contact among the community members partaking of the meal and, thus, also confirmed their common identity perhaps by exclusion of any outsiders or certain social groups like slaves, women, or non-citizens (as in Mylonopoulos 2006: 70, 77, 79, 83-4; Nielsen 2014: 11-12; Rüpke 2012: 314).

Perhaps rather than boundaries, the physical terrain on which the sanctuary complex is spread could have created a ritual topography with pathways through which the community members moved around, perhaps in processions, went into or out of places like the cave and its presumed external extension on the fifth terrace or the temple building on the first terrace, congregated, and dispersed. Therefore, such formal patterns of movement did not only link the ritual components of the sanctuary complex itself. They also brought the community members into a sort of relationship which shaped their ritual experience through both their encounter with the sanctuary itself and their communal ritual performance there. In a sense, the power of certain rites may have derived precisely from their enactment within or around the sanctuary complex. Thus, both sanctuary itself (as a sacred space) and ritual might have been central to the way they, as a community, perceived themselves and their roles and attached meaning to them. In other words, their perception of who they were and what was expected of them might have been shaped by – and, to a certain extent, might have also shaped – their participation in the rituals (as in Edmonds 1999: 7-8, 134, 145; Mylonopoulos 2006: 70, 109).

Chapter 4

4.1 Closure of the site

The sanctuary at Ras il-Wardija seems to have remained in use for a relatively short span of centuries when compared, for instance, to Tas-Silġ in Malta. They could have been the site's own enduring material qualities (or the site's very materiality) – the fact that, for a substantial part, the site seems to have consisted of rock-cut features – that may have largely constrained many subsequent alterations and, thus, hindered a longer use. In simpler terms, because of the nature of its materiality, the site may have not been deemed worth remodelling for long in order to conform to newly-arising demands. It does not necessarily mean that resources or the organisational infrastructure did not exist. But, on the other hand, it might have been very costly and, in certain instances, perhaps physically very difficult to modify rock-cut features. This situation may have rendered the lack of adaptation tolerable only for a while but not for too many centuries (as in Wandsnider 2004: 77).

The material qualities of the Ras il-Wardija site have, therefore, affected the durability of the site's use but, likewise, affected the human activities taking place there. After the creation of the sanctuary, the site was maintained and used for an unknown duration of time; presumably, a relatively short one. But when the site as a working / worshipping and living space could no longer accommodate human activities and no alterations could be made, it is very likely to have been no longer maintained and, thus, was left to decay (as in Wandsnider 2004: 78). In this way, the site's material qualities may have been responsible – or, at least, were among those factors responsible – for the presumed relatively short life-span of both human activity on the site and of the site itself.

4.2 Concluding observations

The connection of the headland sanctuary at Ras il-Wardija with the sea is almost unquestionable on the basis of what has been elaborated. It was this maritime connection which, perhaps sometime around the 3rd century BC, seems to have led towards the building of a small temple on the promontory's edge and the creation of a ritual complex further up on the same promontory possibly by a maritime community whose needs (perhaps along with those of the local agricultural community) it may have served. Certain archaic traits, particularly those betrayed by the small temple, may themselves suggest that they survived longer in rural and / or secluded environments like that where the Ras il-Wardija sanctuary is located.

Therefore, the practised cults seem to have extended from the first to the fifth terrace, both of which hosted the two main units of the sanctuary. On the first terrace, the small temple seems to have consisted of a simple quadrangular structure surrounded by a shallow *temenos* wall. On the fifth terrace, the ritual complex consisted of an artificial cave cut in the rock-face and a presumed built extension that seems to have been later added to it on the front. Both cave and presumed external extension could have played the role of a *telesterion* / initiatory shrine hosting mystery celebrations (see Bianchi 1976: 13. Also 3.9 above) that included ritual banquets, possibly in a hierarchical arrangement. These would seem to have been preceded by cleansing or initiation rituals performed at the nearby rock-cut basin or pool. Processions along the remaining terraces may have also formed part of the practised cults. Syncretised versions of these cults or mystery celebrations could have been also practised by 'hybrid Christians' who may have frequented the sanctuary at Ras il-Wardija in the last years of its use.

But the practised cult or cults seem to have remained aniconic throughout as aniconism is evidenced on both first and fifth terraces while no statues / statuettes (even in fragments) are reported to have been found by the excavators. The deity in the temple on the first terrace was worshipped in the guise of a pyramidal betyl while a cylindrical or column-shaped betyl represented a deity worshipped on the fifth terrace next to the entrance of the presumed cave's external extension until both betyl and its associated offering table had to make way for a later extension to the rock-cut 'pavement' and 'bench' (reclining couch) in the relative area. The engraved figures in the cave are semi-figural or quasi-aniconic, perhaps reflecting a transitional stage from aniconism to iconism. The latter may have been also associated with a cult possibly related to Dionysos (see also below) and might have been carved in a later stage of their hosting cave's lifetime. Notwithstanding this, iconic or image-centred cults were contemporaneously also practised on other sites like Tas-Silġ in Malta (*MISSIONE 1963-70*) showing that, on the Maltese islands, both iconism and aniconism remained in vogue contemporaneously (as in Gaifman 2012: 132).

For people who, like those frequenting the Ras il-Wardija sanctuary (possibly traders or seafarers but, perhaps, even farmers), are closely attached to nature, be it land or sea, religion is a mechanism by which nature and its creative forces are deified. Such people would devote themselves to these both in formal rituals and in their daily attitudes towards them. Thus, one may comprehend why communities amongst whom nature (and its products) is essential for their economy and / or their livelihoood recognise the importance of nature deities, be they sea deities or agricultural deities (Stanislawski 1975: 433, 442).

In view of this, there could have been more than one deity venerated at Ras il-Wardija. One of these might have been Dionysos, his Punic counterpart Shadrapa or, perhaps, both of them in assimilation with each other and who could be also venerated in aniconic form. One should not be surprised to find a cult of Dionysos in Gozo. Identified with wine, Dionysos was also a deity approached in respect of agricultural fertility as was his female counterpart Demeter (or her Roman counterpart Ceres) who was identified with grain / bread (Spaeth 1996: 16, 38) and is shown to have been venerated in Gozo too (*CIL*, X, 7501). During the Roman imperial period, both deities were also considered as deities of the countryside (Spaeth 1996: 28-9) and their cults could be in continuation of earlier locally-established ones retained by the Roman authorities as *municipalia sacra* (municipal cults), as the Romans often did in their *municipia* (De Cazanove 2000: 73). Gozo and Malta were also themselves Roman *municipia* (*CIL*, X, 7495, 7502, 7506-8, 8318). It is no wonder, therefore, that both Ceres and Dionysos enjoyed popularity amongst most ancient Mediterranean societies, particularly the rural and agricultural communities (like that in Gozo) for whom agricultural fertility is expected to have been one of the major concerns and where, thus, it would seem highly unlikely to have one deity's cult without having also the other's. In fact, along with Kore / Persephone (the Greek counterpart of the Roman Proserpina whose cult is also attested in Malta (*CIL*, X, 7494)), Dionysos and Demeter (the Greek counterpart of the Roman Ceres) were worshipped together in Eleusis (in West Attica, Greece), Sicily, and Magna Graecia (Southern Italy) from where their worship reached Rome as a triadic cult of Liber (Dionysos), Ceres, and Libera (Kore / Persephone) (Nielsen 2014: 199(footnote 16)).

But the god Dionysos was also associated with sea-borne trade and traders (see 2.4 above). The probable contact with people from overseas (see 2.4, 3.2 above) occurs at a time when long-distance travelling was far less common than it is nowadays. This fact may have added prestige to places like Ras il-Wardija that may have possibly hosted people from far-off places and brought them into contact with each other as well as with the local people (as in Azzopardi 2014: 154). At the same time, separating it from the mundane environment of any nearby settlements, the sanctuary's peripheral location might have helped to secure an aura of sacredness and ritual cleanliness (as in Guettel Cole 1994: 216; Mather 2003: 27, 36; Prent 2003: 87; Steinsapir 1999: 192). Furthermore, the performance of rituals in such a peripheral location might have also reflected the exodus to the mountains (themselves a peripheral location) as part of maenadic rituals associated with Dionysos like those in ancient Greece and Asia Minor (Nielsen 2014: 208-9). The sanctuary at Ras il-Wardija seems, therefore, to have enjoyed both centrality on account of its possible role as a central meeting place and also marginality due to its geographical location in respect to any associated settlements.

Appendix I

As a sequel to the proposed mysteries possibly celebrated at Ras il-Wardija, it would not be out of place to address also the following question: were there any other mysteries practised in the Maltese islands? What might be a useful hint seems to be provided by a funerary monument the present whereabouts of which are unknown but it has, fortunately, been documented.

The funerary monument was set up to the memory of a young deceased girl and was discovered at 'Rabato, Notabile' (in Malta) around 1725 (Caruana 1882: 117). It is not known which part of 'Rabato' this monument came from but, having been of a funerary nature, one may safely assume that it originated from the part of 'Rabato' that in Classical antiquity formed the cemetery area beyond the walls of Melite (today's Mdina and part of today's Rabat) in conformity with what was prescribed by Table 10 in the Law of the 12 Tables which did not permit burials or cremations in a city / town (Mellor 2013: 4; Toynbee 1996: 48).

Possibly dating to the late Roman occupation of Malta (Azzopardi 2017: 36, 38-9), this monument was erected by the deceased girl's loving mother (see inscription's text and translation below). The monument was pictorially documented in its entirety by means of a sketch (Figure 55) now preserved at the Hermitage in St Petersburg in Russia and where it was recently detected by Mr Daniel Cilia. The sketch served as a preparatory drawing to form part of a lithograph published by Jean Hoüel (1787, pl. CCLXI) wherein, for some reason, a framed inscription that formed part of the said monument was omitted.

The inscription that complemented the monument (but was omitted in the lithograph) reads as follows: *D(is) M(anibus) / Publiciae Glycerae / F(iliae) Su<a>e carissimae / et Pientissimae quae / VIXIT ANNIS XV DIEBUS XXV VIRGI(NE) / BENE MERENTE FECIT PUBLICIA / IRENE MATER*. In translation, it reads: To the gods Manes / Publicia Irene, the mother, well deservedly erected (this monument) to Publicia Glycera, her dearest and most affectionate daughter, who lived as a maiden for 15 years and 25 days.

Occupying the central part of the lithograph (Figure 56) where it is flanked by another funerary monument and architectural specimens, the monument in question shows a female figure seated within a scallop shell flanked by two fluted pilasters and topped by a simple tympanum forming an aedicular shrine beneath which stood the inscription omitted in the lithograph but included in its preparatory drawing (Figure 55). The seated female figure carries what looks to be a tablet in her hands while what appears to be a *cista* (cylindrical basket) stands next to her feet. They seem to have been items associated with her or which could have visually represented personal qualities that she might have been identified with.

Understandably, the seated female figure represents Publicia Glycera over whose tomb the monument is expected to have stood. While the scallop shell (whether in a Christian or a non-Christian context) may be indicative of the girl's (or her family's) beliefs in an afterlife, the *cista* may be indicative of her religious associations in her lifetime.

In Classical iconography, the scallop shell was a symbol of birth or re-birth (Werness 2004: 359). But when associated with burials, the scallop shell could have symbolised re-birth in the context of death. Early Christians, for example, regarded death as the moment of true birth (see Cooley 2012: 62, 231). Therefore, in funerary contexts, the scallop shell might have signified re-birth (through death) to a new life as it might have done when portraits of deceased are shown within a scallop shell on both Christian and non-Christian sarcophagi and other funerary monuments. It is presumably also with this meaning that scallop shells are sometimes found deposited in burials as part of the funerary repertoire accompanying the deceased (see, for example, Ciurana *et al.* 2013). This same meaning or belief is evidently manifested in the execution of our monument and in the symbolism it employs.

In a religious or quasi-religious context (like a funerary context), the image of a *cista* could have been a representation of a *cista mystica*. A *cista mystica* was a cylindrical basket or container and was a common

Figure 55. The entire funerary monument set up to the memory of a young deceased girl by her mother. Discovered at 'Rabato, Notabile' in Malta around 1725, the (late) Roman funerary monument (including its inscription) was pictorially documented in its entirety by means of this sketch / preparatory drawing now preserved at the Hermitage in St Petersburg, Russia. (Photo courtesy: The Hermitage, St Petersburg and Daniel Cilia).

symbol of mysteries (Bremmer 2014: 92, 104; Edmonds III 2013: 357; Nilsson 1985: 96, 143. For the use of the *cista mystica* in initiations into mysteries, see also Bianchi 1976: 36(86), Plate 86; Bremmer 2014: 91; Nilsson 1985: 78-9(Fig. 11), 81). It was used in mysteries to hold items connected with the related mysteries (Bremmer 2014: 92, 108). Even children could be initiated into mysteries, particularly Dionysiac / Bacchic mysteries (see Nilsson 1985: 106-11, 115, 132, 146). When a *cista mystica* is shown in association with a person, it may imply that the person concerned might have been initiated into mysteries while the appearance of the *cista mystica* on a funerary monument may further imply that the mysteries into which the deceased person was initiated (in his / her lifetime) belonged to a chthonic / underworld deity. One such chthonic deity was Persephone / Proserpina (Herodotus, *The Histories* 7. 153 cited in Bowden 2010: 78, 231; Nilsson 1985: 120) who, in Malta, was worshipped in a temple on Mtarfa hill near 'Rabato' where our monument was found. Persephone / Proserpina's cult on Mtarfa hill is evidenced by an inscription found there (*CIL*, X, 7494).

On the other hand, the flat object in the hands of the seated figure on our funerary monument is less easily identifiable. In the presence of the *cista*, however, this intriguing object could have been one of

Figure 56. The funerary monument set up to the memory of a young deceased girl by her mother in the lithograph published by Jean Hoüel. In this lithograph, the monument is seen flanked by another funerary monument and architectural specimens but, for some reason, its inscription is omitted. (Source: Hoüel 1787: Plate CCLXI).

the contents of the *cista* in the form of a tablet from which the seated figure might be reading. During initiations (into mysteries) and mysteries, sacred texts, instructions, or myths related to the deity to whom the mysteries belonged used to be read from scrolls, books, or tablets (as in Bowden 2010: 140; Bremmer 2014: 68, 85, 96, 105, 119; Nilsson 1985: 116-8, 126, 143. See also Bianchi 1976: 36-7(90), Plate 90; Edmonds III 2013: 140-2, 353; Nilsson 1985: 68(Fig. 10a), 74-5) which, on account of their role in mysteries, might have been kept inside the *cista mystica* (see Bremmer 2014: 92, 96, 108). Thus, when shown in combination with a *cista mystica* and in association with an individual, such a scroll, book, or tablet could have not only further indicated the individual's initiation into mysteries but, perhaps, also his / her active participation in the initiation ceremony through his / her reading of the sacred texts or deity-related myths. It is also to be noted that several mystery cults (like, for instance, that of Dionysos in certain places) also held belief in an afterlife as part of their central doctrine (Bremmer 2014: 78-9; Edmonds III 2013: 268-9; Nilsson 1985: 118-32, 143-4, 146-7. See also Bianchi 1976: 5-6, 11, 14; Edmonds III 2013: 248-51). This same belief seems to be also expressed on our funerary monument (see above).

The religious identity of the deceased (and of her family) shown on our monument is difficult to be determined precisely (Azzopardi 2017: 38-40). Nonetheless, as in times of transition, embracing Christianity while remaining attached to non-Christian mysteries could be a widespread phenomenon. Thus, in late Roman times, initiation or participation in mysteries could be familiar amongst Christians and non-Christians alike.

Appendix II

Human skeletal remains were also found at Ras il-Wardija during the excavations by the *Missione Archeologica Italiana a Malta* from 1964 to 1967. These skeletal remains are now preserved in storage at the Gozo Archaeology Museum in the Citadel (Victoria) where they have been always kept alongside the other material from the said excavations. A label accompanying the bones replaces an earlier one which likewise gave Ras il-Wardija as their provenance. For some reason, however, the bones are not given any mention in the *Missione*'s preliminary report which is the only site excavation report published to date (see 1.2 above).

The bones are in a very fragmentary state, perhaps due to the type of terrain they were buried in. As they are not accompanied by any material finds, it is assumed that the bones were found on their own, perhaps in isolation. Moreover, as they were left out completely from the *Missione*'s preliminary report, one also suspects that the human bones found buried there were not considered by the excavators to be of any archaeological value or to have had anything to do with the archaeological site.

Some observations can, nonetheless, be afforded. The site (i.e. Ras il-Wardija) is not known to have been a burial ground either in antiquity or in later times. No other burials are known from the immediate surroundings of the site either. The burial was, therefore, in isolation. As indicated above, the burial might have been also relatively recent or, at least, more recent than the occupation of the archaeological site in antiquity.

Taken into consideration, these factors may instigate certain questions: Did the individual die on that spot and was buried there? But why buried there, in that remote place? The circumstances of the burial might be indicative of a discreet burial. Discreet burials are normally associated with murders where the victim is discreetly buried to hide any evidence. Is it, therefore, an instance concerning a murder victim whose case remained unresolved?

Available information, in fact, seems to point in this direction. Remaining anonymous, an informant recalls that, when news of the find reached the neighbouring localities, word soon spread among the local elderly confirming their conviction that the discovered remains belonged to a man whom most of them knew and whose fatal incident they still remembered, including the location details. Yet, they never divulged anything.

The incident had taken place around fifty or sixty years earlier; so, it must have been around the beginning of the 20th century. The man went fishing from the cliffs at Ras il-Wardija where he and another fisherman confronted each other over a fishing spot. The confrontation escalated, turned violent, and ended up in murder. The man (who was the victim) was discreetly buried on the spot never to be heard of again. His disappearance remained unresolved until his bones were brought to light during the excavations conducted by the *Missione* at Ras il-Wardija. The find, however, was kept at low profile. It was not even mentioned in the *Missione*'s preliminary report referred to above.

Bibliography

Abbreviated titles

CIL *Corpus Inscriptionum Latinarum* (Berlin, 1853-).

CIS *Corpus Inscriptionum Semiticarum* (Paris, 1881-1961).

Libr *Library*

LIMC *Lexicon Iconographicum Mythologiae Classicae* (Zurich and Munich, 1981-2009).

MISSIONE *Missione Archeologica Italiana a Malta. Rapporto Preliminare della Campagna 1963-70* (Roma, 1964-73).

MAR *Museum Annual Reports* (Malta, 1905-2002).

MS *Manuscript*

NLM *National Library of Malta*

Report 1961 & 1970 *Report by Imperial College Archaeological Expedition on the Roman Wrecks at Xlendi Gozo. 1961 & 1970.* Unpublished typescript, National Museum of Archaeology (Malta) Library, DAG·16·9, TS(115).

Ancient sources

Apollonius Rhodius, *The Argonautica*

Apuleius, *The Golden Ass*

Clement of Alexandria, *Exhortation to the Greeks*

Demosthenes, *On the Crown*

Diodorus Siculus, *Library of History*

Euripides, *Cretans*

Flavius Josephus, *Against Apion*

Herodotus, *The Histories*

John (Biblical Gospel of)

Jonah (Biblical Old Testament book of)

Macrobius, *Saturnalia*

Nonnus, *Dionysiaca*

Numbers (Biblical Old Testament book of)

Pausanias, *Description of Greece*

Plutarch, *On Isis and Osiris*

Porphyrius, *On the Cave of the Nymphs*

Psalms (Biblical Old Testament book of)

Thucydides, *History of the Peloponnesian War*

Virgil, *Georgics*

Digital sources

EdgarLOwen.com
http://www.auac.ch/iap/season2010/iap_2010_text03a.html
https://www.bing.com/images
www.geocities.ws/maltashells/NatHist.html
pierluigimontalbano.blogspot.com.mt/2015/04/archeologia-e-scrittura-i-triangoli.html
shari-chocolatebox.blogspot.com/2011/02/fatimas-protection.html

Published works

Agius de Soldanis, G. P. F. 1750. *Della Lingua Punica presentemente usata da Maltesi*. Facsimile edition, 2007. Malta, Joe Zammit Ciantar.

Akar Tanriver, D. S. 2015. Bull / Bovine Figurines from the Sanctuary of Apollo Clarius (Ionia). In A. Muller, E. Lafli, and S. Huysecom-Haxhi (eds.), *Figurines de terre cuite en Méditerranée grecque et romaine*, 2. Iconographie et contexts: 125-36. Villeneuve d'Ascq (France), Presses Universitaires du Septentrion.

Ascough, R. S., Harland, P. A. and Kloppenborg, J. S. 2012. *Associations in the Greco-Roman World. A Sourcebook.* Waco (Texas), Baylor University Press and De Gruyter.

Atauz, A. D. 2004. *Trade, Piracy, and Naval Warfare in the Central Mediterranean: The Maritime History and Archaeology of Malta*. Online PhD thesis, Texas A&M University.

Aulisa, I. 2014. I Santuari visti dal mare: L'Adriatico nel Portolano Sacro. In I. Aulisa (ed.), *I Santuari e il Mare*. Atti del III Convegno Internazionale, Santuario Santa Maria di Monte Berico, Vicenza, 15-17 aprile 2013: 111-48. Bari, Edipuglia.

Azzopardi, E. 2013. The Shipwrecks of Xlendi Bay, Gozo, Malta. *The International Journal of Nautical Archaeology* 42/2 (2013): 286-95.

Azzopardi, E., Gambin, T. and Zerafa, R. 2013. Ancient anchors from Malta and Gozo. *Malta Archaeological Review* 9 (2008-2009): 22-31.

Azzopardi, G. 2007. *The Extramural Necropolis of Gaulos*. Gozo, The Author.

Azzopardi, G. 2012. Antiquarian and Connoisseur: putting Gozo's Archaeological Legacy in the Limelight. In G. Vella and O. Vella (eds.), *De Soldanis: an eighteenth century intellectual*: 55-72. Malta, Heritage Malta.

Azzopardi, G. 2014. *Religious Landscapes and Identities of the Maltese Islands in a Mediterranean Context: 700 BC – AD 500*. Online Ph.D. thesis, Durham University.

Azzopardi, G. 2017. Religious identity and perceptions of afterlife gleaned from a funerary monument to a young girl from (late) Roman Melite. *Malta Archaeological Review* 11 (2012-2013): 34-40.

Bender, B. 1993. Landscape – meaning and action. In B. Bender (ed.), *Landscape: Politics and Perspectives*: 1-17. Providence / Oxford, Berg Publishers.

Bianchi, U. 1976. *The Greek Mysteries*. Iconography of Religions XVII, 3. Leiden, E.J. Brill.

Bonanno, A. (with Cilia, D.) 2005. *Malta. Phoenician, Punic and Roman*. Malta, Midsea Books Ltd.

Bowden, H. 2010. *Mystery Cults in the Ancient World*. London, Thames & Hudson Ltd.

Bradley, R. 1991. Monuments and places. In P. Garwood, D. Jennings, R. Skeates and J. Toms (eds.), *Sacred and Profane*. Proceedings of a Conference on Archaeology, Ritual and Religion. Oxford, 1989: 135-40. Oxford, Oxford Committee for Archaeology, Institute of Archaeology.

Bradley, R. 2000. *An Archaeology of Natural Places*. London, Routledge.

Bradley, R. 2002. *The Past in Prehistoric Societies*. London and New York, Routledge.

Brakke, D. 2015. From Temple to Cell, from Gods to Demons: Pagan Temples in the Monastic Topography of Fourth-Century Egypt. In J. Hahn, S. Emmel and U. Gotter (eds.), *From Temple to Church. Destruction and Renewal of Local Cultic Topography in Late Antiquity*: 91-112. Leiden / Boston, Brill.

Bremmer, J. N. 2014. *Initiation into the Mysteries of the Ancient World*. Berlin and Boston, De Gruyter.

Briault, C. 2007. Making mountains out of molehills in the Bronze age Aegean: visibility, ritual kits, and the idea of a peak sanctuary. *World Archaeology* 39/1: 122-41.

Brody, A. J. 1998. *'Each Man cried out to his God'. The Specialised Religion of Canaanite and Phoenician Seafarers*. Harvard Semitic Monographs, 58. Atlanta (GA), Scholars Press.

Budin, S. L. 2014. Before Kypris was Aphrodite. In D. T. Sugimoto (ed.), *Transformation of a Goddess. Ishtar – Astarte – Aphrodite*. Orbis Biblicus et Orientalis, 263: 195-215. Fribourg and Göttingen, Academic Press Fribourg and Vandenhoeck & Ruprecht.

Buhagiar, M. 2014. *Essays on the Archaeology and Ancient History of the Maltese Islands: Bronze Age to Byzantine*. Malta, Midsea Books Ltd.

Burkert, W. 2012. Ancient Views on Festivals. A Case of Near Eastern Mediterranean Koine. In J. Rasmus Brandt and J. W. Iddeng (eds.), *Greek and Roman Festivals. Content, Meaning, and Practice*: 39-51. Oxford, Oxford University Press.

Caruana, A. A. 1882. *Report on the Phoenician and Roman antiquities in the group of the islands of Malta*. Malta.

Champeaux, J. 2002. *La Religione dei Romani* (trans. by Graziella Zattoni Nesi). Universale paperbacks il Mulino, 419. Bologna, Società editrice il Mulino.

Chaniotis, A. 2015. The Conversion of the Temple of Aphrodite at Aphrodisias in Context. In J. Hahn, S. Emmel and U. Gotter (eds.), *From Temple to Church. Destruction and Renewal of Local Cultic Topography in Late Antiquity*: 243-73. Leiden / Boston, Brill.

Ciurana, J., Provinciale, E. and Salagaray, M. 2013. *El Área Funeraria del Suburbio Oriental de Tarraco (Siglos I-III d.C.)*. Poster presented at the 18th International Congress of Classical Archaeology 'Centre and periphery in the ancient world', Merida, 13-17 May 2013.

Cooley, A. E. 2012. *The Cambridge Manual of Latin Epigraphy*. New York, Cambridge University Press.

Crooks, S. 2013. *What are these Queer Stones? Baetyls: Epistemology of a Minoan Fetish*. British Archaeological Reports International Series, 2511. Oxford, Archaeopress.

Crumley, C. L. 1999. Sacred landscapes: constructed and conceptualized. In W. Ashmore and A. B. Knapp (eds.), *Archaeologies of Landscape: Contemporary Perspectives*: 269-76. Oxford, Blackwell Publishers Ltd.

Curzi, G. 2012. I graffiti figurativi: una lettura simbolica. In C. Tedeschi (ed.), *Graffiti templari. Scritture e simboli medievali in una tomba etrusca di Tarquinina*: 115-54. Roma, Viella.

De Cazanove, O. 2000. Some Thoughts on the 'Religious Romanisation' of Italy before the Social War (trans. by Edward Bispham). In E. Bispham and C. Smith (eds.), *Religion in Archaic and Republican Rome and Italy. Evidence and Experience*: 71-6. Chicago and London, Fitzroy Dearborn Publishers.

Delattre, A. L. 1906. *Une visite à la Nécropole des Rabs prêtres et prêtresses de Carthage*. Palermo, Stabilimento Tipografico Virzi.

Demetriou, D. 2012. *Negotiating Identity in the Ancient Mediterranean. The Archaic and Classical Greek Multiethnic Emporia*. New York, Cambridge University Press.

Des Bouvrie, S. 2012. Greek Festivals and the Ritual Process. An Inquiry into the Olympia-cum-Heraia and the Great Dionysia. In J. Rasmus Brandt and J. W. Iddeng (eds.), *Greek and Roman Festivals. Content, Meaning, and Practice*: 53-93. Oxford, Oxford University Press.

De Vincenzo, S. 2013. *Tra Cartagine e Roma. I centri urbani dell' eparchia punica di Sicilia tra VI e I sec. a.C.* Berlin / Boston, De Gruyter.

Edmonds, M. 1999. *Ancestral Geographies of the Neolithic: Landscape, Monuments and Memory*. London, Routledge.

Edmonds III, R. G. 2013. *Redefining Ancient Orphism. A Study in Greek Religion*. Cambridge, Cambridge University Press.

Emmel, S., Gotter, U. and Hahn, J. 2015. 'From Temple to Church': Analysing a Late Antique Phenomenon of Transformation. In J. Hahn, S. Emmel and U. Gotter (eds.), *From Temple to Church. Destruction and Renewal of Local Cultic Topography in Late Antiquity*: 1-22. Leiden / Boston, Brill.

Evans, A. J. 1901. Mycenean Tree and Pillar Cult and Its Mediterranean Relations. *The Journal of Hellenic Studies* 21: 99-204.

Evans, J. D. 1971. *The Prehistoric Antiquities of the Maltese Islands: A Survey*. London, The Athlone Press (University of London).

Fiorini, S. and Mallia-Milanes, V. (eds.) 1991. *Malta: A Case Study in International Cross-Currents*. Proceedings of the First International Colloquium on the history of the Central Mediterranean held at the University of Malta, 13-17 December 1989. Malta, Malta University Publications, Malta Historical Society, and Foundation for International Studies (University of Malta).

Foucher, L. 1966. Un sanctuaire néo punique à Menzel Harb. In *Africa*: 119-30. Tunis, Secrétariat d'etat aux affaires culturelles.

Frankfurter, D. 2015. Iconoclasm and Christianization in Late Antique Egypt: Christian Treatments of Space and Image. In J. Hahn, S. Emmel and U. Gotter (eds.), *From Temple to Church. Destruction and Renewal of Local Cultic Topography in Late Antiquity*: 135-59. Leiden / Boston, Brill.

Gaifman, M. 2012. *Aniconism in Greek Antiquity*. Oxford Studies in Ancient Culture and Representation. Oxford, Oxford University Press.

Galdi, A. 2014. Navigazioni e Devozioni nel XV secolo: Il Mar Tirreno nel *Portulano dei Santi*. In I. Aulisa (ed.), *I Santuari e il Mare*. Atti del III Convegno Internazionale, Santuario Santa Maria di Monte Berico, Vicenza, 15-17 aprile 2013: 149-66. Bari, Edipuglia.

Gambin, T. 2003. Islands of the Middle Sea: an archaeology of a coastline. In L. De Maria and R. Turchetti (eds.), *Evolución Paleoambiental de los Puertos y Fondeaderos Antiguos en el Mediterráneo Occidental*. I Seminarìo el Patrimonio Arqueológico Submarino y los Puertos Antiguos, Alicante, 14-15 Noviembre 2003: 127-46. Soveria Mannelli (CZ) – Italy, Rubbettino.

Gambin, T. 2005. The harbours of ancient Gozo. *Malta Archaeological Review* 6: 15-21.

Gambin, T. 2010. Maritime links of chapels dedicated to St Paul in the Maltese islands. In J. Azzopardi and A. Pace (eds.), *St Paul in Malta and the shaping of a nation's identity*: 145-59. Malta, Office of the Prime Minister.

Ghey, E. 2007. Empty spaces or meaningful places? A broader perspective on continuity. In R. Haeussler and A. C. King (eds.), *Continuity and Innovation in Religion in the Roman West* I. Journal of Roman Archaeology Supplementary Series, 67: 19-30. Portsmouth (Rhode Island), Journal of Roman Archaeology.

Gleba, M. 2009. Textile tools in ancient Italian votive contexts: evidence of dedication or production? In M. Gleba and H. Becker (eds.), *Votives, Places and Rituals in Etruscan Religion*. Studies in Honor of Jean MacIntosh Turfa: 69-84. Leiden / Boston, Brill.

Glinister, F. 2000. Sacred Rubbish. In E. Bispham and C. Smith (eds.), *Religion in Archaic and Republican Rome and Italy. Evidence and Experience*: 54-70. Chicago and London, Fitzroy Dearborn Publishers.

Gordon, S. 2015. Domestic magic and the walking dead in medieval England: A diachronic approach. In C. Houlbrook and N. Armitage (eds.), *The Materiality of Magic. An artefactual investigation into ritual practices and popular beliefs*: 65-84. Oxford and Philadelphia, Oxbow Books.

Guettel Cole, S. 1994. Demeter in the ancient Greek city and its countryside. In S. E. Alcock and R. Osborne (eds.), *Placing the Gods: Sanctuaries and Sacred Space in Ancient Greece*: 199-216. New York, Oxford University Press Inc.

Harding, J. 1991. Using the unique as the typical: monuments and the ritual landscape. In P. Garwood, D. Jennings, R. Skeates and J. Toms (eds.), *Sacred and Profane*. Proceedings of a Conference on Archaeology, Ritual and Religion. Oxford, 1989: 141-51. Oxford, Oxford Committee for Archaeology, Institute of Archaeology.

Henrichs, A. 1993. 'He Has a God in Him': Human and Divine in the Modern Perception of Dionysus. In T. H. Carpenter and C. A. Faraone (eds.), *Masks of Dionysus*: 13-43. Ithaca and London, Cornell University Press.

Horsnaes, H. 2002. Lucanian sanctuaries and cultural interaction. In P. Attema, G. J. Burgers, E. Van Joolen, M. Van Leusen and B. Mater (eds.), *New Developments in Italian Landscape Archaeology*. British Archaeological Reports International Series, 1091: 229-34. Oxford, Archaeopress.

Hoüel, J. 1787. *Voyage Pittoresque des Isles de Sicile, de Lipari et de Malte* IV. Paris.

Iddeng, J. W. 2012. What is a Graeco-Roman Festival? A Polythetic Approach. In J. Rasmus Brandt and J. W. Iddeng (eds.), *Greek and Roman Festivals. Content, Meaning, and Practice*: 11-37. Oxford, Oxford University Press.

Jaccarini, C. J. and Cauchi, M. N. 1999. The enigmatic rock-cut pans of Mġarr ix-Xini. *Melita Historica* 12/4: 419-44.

Jameson, M. 1993. The Asexuality of Dionysus. In T. H. Carpenter and C. A. Faraone (eds.), *Masks of Dionysus*: 44-64. Ithaca and London, Cornell University Press.

Jost, M. 1994. The distribution of sanctuaries in civic space in Arkadia. In S. E. Alcock and R. Osborne (eds.), *Placing the Gods: Sanctuaries and Sacred Space in Ancient Greece*: 217-30. New York, Oxford University Press Inc.

Kearns, E. 2010. *Ancient Greek Religion. A Sourcebook*. West Sussex, Wiley-Blackwell.

Kerényi, C. 1976. *DIONYSOS. Archetypal Image of Indestructible Life* (trans. by Ralph Manheim). New Jersey, Princeton University Press.

Kerényi, C. 1980. *The Gods of the Greeks*. New York, Thames & Hudson.

Lahiri, N. 1996. Archaeological landscapes and textual images: a study of the sacred geography of late medieval Ballabgarh. *World Archaeology* 28/2: 244-64.

Larson, J. 2007. *Ancient Greek Cults. A Guide*. New York and London, Routledge.

Lauter, H. 1979. Bemerkungen zur späthellenistischen Baukunst in Mittelitalien. *JdI* 94 (1979): 390-459.

Malkin, I. 1987. *Religion and Colonization in Ancient Greece*. Leiden, E.J. Brill.

Malone, C., Bonanno, A., Trump, D., Dixon, J., Leighton, R., Pedley, M., Stoddart, S. and Schembri, P. J. 2009. Material Culture. In C. Malone, S. Stoddart, A. Bonanno and D. Trump (with T. Gouder and A. Pace) (eds.), *Mortuary Customs in Prehistoric Malta. Excavations at the Brochtorff Circle at Xagħra (1987-94)*: 219-313. Cambridge, McDonald Institute for Archaeological Research.

Malone, C., Stoddart, S., Trump, D. and Duhig, C. 2009. Żebbuġ Phase Levels: Spatial and Stratigraphic Analysis. In C. Malone, S. Stoddart, A. Bonanno and D. Trump (with T. Gouder and A. Pace) (eds.), *Mortuary Customs in Prehistoric Malta. Excavations at the Brochtorff Circle at Xagħra (1987-94)*: 95-107. Cambridge, McDonald Institute for Archaeological Research.

Marangou, C. 2001. Sacred or secular places and the ambiguous evidence of prehistoric rituals. In P. F. Biehl, F. Bertemes and H. Meller (eds.), *The Archaeology of Cult and Religion*: 139-60. Budapest, Archaeolingua Foundation.

Mather, C. 2003. Shrines and the domestication of landscape. *Journal of Anthropological Research* 59/1: 23-45.

Mattingly, D. (with Edwards, D.) 2003. Religious and Funerary Structures. In D. J. Mattingly (ed.), *The Archaeology of Fazzān. Synthesis* 1, Society for Libyan Studies Monograph, 5: 177-234. London and Tripoli, The Society for Libyan Studies and Department of Antiquities, Socialist People's Libyan Arab Jamahariya.

Mattingly, D. J. (ed.) 2007. *The Archaeology of Fazzān. Site Gazetteer, Pottery and other Survey Finds* 2, Society for Libyan Studies Monograph, 7. London and Tripoli, The Society for Libyan Studies and Department of Antiquities, Socialist People's Libyan Arab Jamahariya.

McNiven, I. J. 2003. Saltwater People: Spiritscapes, Maritime Rituals and the Archaeology of Australian Indigenous Seascapes. *World Archaeology* 35/3: 329-49.

Mellor, R. 2013. *The Historians of Ancient Rome. An Anthology of the Major Writings*. 3rd edn. London and New York, Routledge.

Morford, M. P. O. and Lenardon, R. J. 1999. *Classical Mythology*. 6th edn. Oxford and New York, Oxford University Press.

Morgan, C. 1994. The evolution of a sacral 'landscape': Isthmia, Perachora, and the early Corinthian state. In S. E. Alcock and R. Osborne (eds.), *Placing the Gods: Sanctuaries and Sacred Space in Ancient Greece*: 105-42. New York, Oxford University Press Inc.

Moscati, S. 2005. *Fenici e Cartaginesi in Sardegna*. Bibliotheca sarda, 102. Nuoro, Ilisso Edizioni.

Mylonopoulos, J. 2006. Greek sanctuaries as places of communication through rituals: an archaeological perspective. In E. Stavrianopoulou (ed.), *Ritual and Communication in the Graeco-Roman World*: 69-110. Liège, Centre International d'Étude de la Religion Grecque Antique.

Nakhai, B. A. 2001. *Archaeology and the Religions of Canaan and Israel*. Boston (MA), American Schools of Oriental Research.

Nielsen, I. 2014. *Housing the Chosen. The Architectural Context of Mystery Groups and Religious Associations in the Ancient World*. Contextualizing the Sacred, 2. Turnhout (Belgium), Brepols Publishers.

Nilsson, M. P. 1985. *The Dionysiac Mysteries of the Hellenistic and Roman Age*. Salem (New Hampshire), Ayer Company, Publishers, Inc.

Obbink, D. 1993. Dionysus Poured Out: Ancient and Modern Theories of Sacrifice and Cultural Formation. In T. H. Carpenter and C. A. Faraone (eds.), *Masks of Dionysus*: 65-86. Ithaca and London, Cornell University Press.

Osborne, R. 2007. Cult and ritual. The Greek world. In S. E. Alcock and R. Osborne (eds.), *Classical Archaeology*: 246-62. Malden, Oxford and Victoria, Blackwell Publishing Ltd.

Parcero Oubina, C., Criado Boado, F. and Santos Estevez, M. 1998. Rewriting landscape: incorporating sacred landscapes into cultural traditions. *World Archaeology* 30/1: 159-76.

Pesce, G. 2000. *Sardegna Punica*. Bibliotheca sarda, 56. Nuoro, Ilisso Edizioni.

Prent, M. 2003. Glories of the Past in the Past: Ritual Activities at Palatial Ruins in Early Iron Age Crete. In R. M. Van Dyke and S. E. Alcock (eds.), *Archaeologies of Memory*: 81-103. Oxford, Blackwell Publishers Ltd.

Radic-Rossi, I. 2005. The Mljet shipwreck, Croatia: Roman glass from the sea. *Minerva* 16/3: 33-5.

Rainbird, P. 2007. *The Archaeology of Islands*. New York, Cambridge University Press.

Rasmus Brandt, J. 2012. Content and Form. Some Considerations on Greek Festivals and Archaeology. In J. Rasmus Brandt and J. W. Iddeng (eds.), *Greek and Roman Festivals. Content, Meaning, and Practice*: 139-98. Oxford, Oxford University Press.

Rüpke, J. 2012. Public and Publicity. Long-Term Changes in Religious Festivals during the Roman Republic. In J. Rasmus Brandt and J. W. Iddeng (eds.), *Greek and Roman Festivals. Content, Meaning, and Practice*: 305-22. Oxford, Oxford University Press.

Sahlqvist, L. 2001. Territorial behaviour and communication in a ritual landscape. *Geografiska Annaler*. Series B (Human Geography) 83/2: 79-102.

Sami, D. 2010. Changing Beliefs: The Transition from Pagan to Christian Town in Late Antique Sicily. In D. Sami and G. Speed (eds.), *Debating Urbanism Within and Beyond the Walls A.D. 300-700*. Proceedings of a conference held at the University of Leicester, 15th November 2008. Leicester Archaeology Monograph, 17: 213-37. Leicester, School of Archaeology & Ancient History, University of Leicester.

Saradi, H. 2015. The Christianization of Pagan Temples in the Greek Hagiographical Texts. In J. Hahn, S. Emmel and U. Gotter (eds.), *From Temple to Church. Destruction and Renewal of Local Cultic Topography in Late Antiquity*: 113-34. Leiden / Boston, Brill.

Scarre, C. 2002. Introduction: situating monuments. The dialogue between built form and landform in Atlantic Europe. In C. Scarre (ed.), *Monuments and Landscape in Atlantic Europe: Perception and Society during the Neolithic and Early Bronze Age*: 1-14. London, Routledge.

Shaw, J. W. and Shaw, M. C. (eds.) 2000. *Kommos IV. The Greek Sanctuary*. Princeton and Oxford, Princeton University Press.

Simon, E. 1962. Dionysischer Sarkophag in Princeton. *Römische Mitteilungen* 69: 136-58.

Sinopoli, C. M. 2003. Echoes of empire: Vijayanagara and historical memory, Vijayanagara as historical memory. In R. M. Van Dyke and S. E. Alcock (eds.), *Archaeologies of Memory*: 17-33. Oxford, Blackwell Publishers Ltd.

Spaeth, B. S. 1996. *The Roman Goddess Ceres*. Austin, University of Texas Press.

Stanislawski, D. 1975. Dionysus westward: early religion and the economic geography of wine. *Geographical Review* 65/4: 427-44.

Steinsapir, A. I. 1999. Landscape and the sacred: the sanctuary dedicated to holy, heavenly Zeus Baetocaece. *Near Eastern Archaeology* 62/3: 182-94.

Stoddart, S. 1999. Long-term dynamics of an island community. Malta 5500 BC – 2000 AD. In R. H. Tykot, J. Morter and J. E. Robb (eds.), *Social Dynamics of the Prehistoric Central Mediterranean*: 137-47. London, Accordia Research Institute, University of London.

Stoddart, S., Malone, C., Mason, S., Trump, B. and Trump, D. 2009. The Tarxien Phase Levels: Spatial and Stratigraphic Analysis and Reconstruction. In C. Malone, S. Stoddart, A. Bonanno and D. Trump (with T. Gouder and A. Pace) (eds.), *Mortuary Customs in Prehistoric Malta. Excavations at the Brochtorff Circle at Xagħra (1987-94)*: 109-205. Cambridge, McDonald Institute for Archaeological Research.

Taylor, R. 2005. Roman Oscilla: An Assessment. *RES: Anthropology and Aesthetics* 48 (Autumn, 2005): 83-105.

Tilley, C. 2004. *The Materiality of Stone: Explorations in Landscape Phenomenology* 1. Oxford / New York, Berg.

Tilley, C. 1996. The powers of rocks: topography and monument construction on Bodmin Moor. *World Archaeology* 28/2: 161-76.

Toynbee, J. M. C. 1996. *Death and Burial in the Roman World*. Baltimore, The Johns Hopkins University Press.

Trump, D. H. (with Cilia, D.) 2004. *Malta: Prehistory and Temples*. 2nd edn. Malta, Midsea Books Ltd.

Trump, D. H. and Mallia, F. S. 1964. *Roman Shipwreck, Xlendi, Gozo*. Unpublished typescript, National Museum of Archaeology (Malta) Library, DAG·16·9, TSS(34).

Valk, H. 2007. Choosing holy places. In R. Haeussler and A. C. King (eds.), *Continuity and Innovation in Religion in the Roman West* I. Journal of Roman Archaeology Supplementary Series, 67: 201-12. Portsmouth (Rhode Island), Journal of Roman Archaeology.

Van Dyke, R. M. and Alcock, S. E. 2003. Archaeologies of memory: an introduction. In R. M. Van Dyke and S. E. Alcock (eds.), *Archaeologies of Memory*: 1-13. Oxford, Blackwell Publishers Ltd.

Vella, C. 2013. *The Mediterranean Artistic Context of Late Medieval Malta, 1091-1530*. Malta, Midsea Books.

Vella, H. C. R. 1993. Fertility Aspects in Ancient North Africa. *Journal of Mediterranean Studies* 3/2: 215-24.

Wandsnider, L. 2004. Artifact, landscape, and temporality in eastern Mediterranean archaeological landscape studies. In E. F. Athanassopoulos and L. Wandsnider (eds.), *Mediterranean Archaeological Landscapes: Current Issues*: 69-79. Philadelphia, University of Pennsylvania Museum of Archaeology and Anthropology.

Wenning, R. 2001. The Betyls of Petra. *BASOR* 324: 79-95.

Wenning, R. and Gorgerat, L. 2014. *The International Aslah Project (IAP): Southern Terrace - a. The Triclinium of Aslah (D. 17). Preliminary report on the 2010 season.* AUAC: 1-11. (Downloaded from http://www.auac.ch/iap/season2010/iap_2010_text03a.html. Accessed: 14-10-2016).

Werness, H. B. 2004. *The Continuum Encyclopedia of Animal Symbolism in Art.* New York, Continuum International Publishing Group.

Zammit Ciantar, J. 2000. *The Placenames of the Coast of Gozo (Malta).* Malta, Privately published.

Zampi, M. 2002. *Il Triclinio. Mito e politica dell'alimentazione nell'antica Roma.* Sassari, Isola Felice.

Zifferero, A. 2002. The geography of the ritual landscape in complex societies. In P. Attema, G. J. Burgers, E. Van Joolen, M. Van Leusen and B. Mater (eds.), *New Developments in Italian Landscape Archaeology.* British Archaeological Reports International Series, 1091: 246-65. Oxford, Archaeopress.

General Index

Abdul, 6–7
Ablution, 38
   Rites, 38
Aegean, 16, 18, 43, 53, 68
   Sea, 53
   Traditions, 43
Africa, 9, 21, 54, 69, 72
Afterlife, 63, 65, 68
Agrarian, 52
   Populations, 52
   Societies, 52
   Year, 52
Agricultural, 1–2, 6–7, 12, 17, 27, 61–62
   Activity, 2, 27
   Community, 61-62
   Deities, 62
   Fertility, 62
Akrokorinth, 34
Alkamenes, 41
Altar, 21, 26, 40, 42, 47
Altars, 13, 26, 40, 57
   Portable, 13
Al-Uzza, 53
Amazon, 47
Amphora, 9, 14
Anchor, 9, 11
   Collar, 9
   Stock, 9, 11
   Stocks, 9, 11
Anchors, 11, 46
Anchorage, 6, 9, 46
Ancillary, 2, 17, 27
   Features, 17, 27
Angevins, 3
Aniconic, 26, 34, 36, 41, 43, 45, 49, 61–62
   Form, 26, 34, 62
   Representation, 34, 43, 45, 49
Aniconism, 50–51, 61–62, 69
Anna Chiara Fariselli, 45
Anne Monsarrat, 8
Anthropomorphic, 13, 49, 51, 60
   Mask, 13
Anthropomorphism, 50
Antique, 54, 69, 71–72
   Late, 54
Antiquity, 4, 9, 40, 42, 51, 60, 63, 66, 68–69, 72
   Classical, 9, 42, 63
   Late, 4
Aphrodite, 45, 53, 68–69
Apollo, 41, 45, 55–56, 68
   Agyieus, 41
   Carinus, 45
   Of the Streets, 41
Apollonius Rhodius, 47, 67
Apotropaic, 12, 14, 42
   Device, 12, 42
   Function, 12
Aragonese, 3–4, 59
   Period, 59
Archaic, 23, 25, 45, 51, 61, 69–70
   Period, 51
   Temple, 23, 25, 45
Architecture, 26, 31
Ares, 47
Arkadian, 41
   Gate, 41
Arretine ware, 35
Ashmolean Museum, 55–56
Asia Minor, 31–32, 41, 60, 62
Aslah, 29, 73
Astarte, 46, 68
Astragal, 11
Athenian acropolis, 41
Athens, 15, 41, 52–53, 55
Atlantic, 21, 72
Attica, 31, 62
   West, 62
Attis, 52
Augustan, 51
Axiokersos, 55–56

Babylon, 41
Babylonian, 41
   Historian, 41
   Priest, 41
Bacchic, 12, 58, 64
   Mysteries, 12, 64
Bacchus, 52, 54–56
   Zagreos, 51–52, 54–55, 58, 60
Bakcheion, 34
Baltimore, 55, 72
Banquet, 34–35, 39, 53
   Ritual, 35, 57, 61
   Sacred, 53
   Symposia-like, 58
Banqueting, 31–35
   Bench, 32
   Hall, 31-33
   Room, 31, 32, 34–35
Baptism, 38, 58–59
Basin, 1, 19, 30, 35–40, 48, 61
Berosus, 41
Betyl, 13, 26, 30, 36, 41–51, 61
   Pyramidal, 26, 43–47, 49, 51, 61
   Column-shaped, 30, 41, 48–49, 51, 61
   Worshipped, 49
Biblical, 41, 58, 67
   Theme, 58
Biclinium, 35
Bir Miftuḥ, 59
Bithia, 23, 25
Black Sea, 47
Bologna, 54
   Museo Civico Archeologico in Bologna, 54
Boston (see: Museum of Fine Arts, Boston)
Boukoloi, 31–32, 52

Bovine, 42, 68
British, 3–4, 69–70, 73
Bronze Age, 3–4, 68, 72
Byzantine, 4, 68
    Empire, 4

Cabras, 45–46
    Archaeological Museum of Cabras, 45–46
Caduceus, 14
Canaan, 58, 71
Capo San Marco, 23, 25, 45
Caria, 41
Carla del Vais, 45
Carthage, 1, 4, 14, 69
Carthaginian, 21, 45–46
Catacomb, 7
    Late Roman, 7
Cathedral, 7
    Museum, 7
Catholic University of Milan, 2
Celestial, 46
    Attributes, 46
    Deity, 46
    Symbols, 46
Cemetery, 4, 63
Centrality, 62
Ceres, 62, 72
Chia, 23, 25
Chi-rho, 58
    Monogram, 58
Chloe, 53
Chous, 55
    Attic, 55
Christ, 41, 58–60
    Crucified, 58–60
Christian, 9, 13–14, 38, 58–60, 63, 65, 69, 72
    Belief, 58
    Celebration, 58
    Context, 63
    Hybrid, 58, 61
    Initiation rite, 38, 58
    Look, 59
    Mystery, 58, 65
    Phenomenon, 58
Christianisation, 58–59
    Process, 58
Christianity, 4, 57–59, 65
    Early, 4, 57
Chronology, 4
    Maltese, 4
Chthonic, 56, 64
    Deity, 56, 64
Cippus, 43–44
Cista, 63–65
    Mystica, 63–65
Citadel, 7, 66
Classical, 6–7, 9, 16, 42, 63, 69, 71
    Antiquity, 9, 42, 63
    Iconography, 63
    Period, 7, 9
    Times, 6–7, 16
Clement of Alexandria, 51, 57, 67
Colonial, 5
    Domination, 5

    Relationship, 5
Column, 13, 30, 34–36, 41, 47–49, 51, 61
Comino, 1, 3
Communal, 31–34, 39, 52–53, 57, 60
    Meal, 32, 52-53, 57, 60
Communication, 7–9, 11, 23, 34, 45, 48, 71–72
    Maritime, 23
Consumption, 8, 52, 58
Corinth, 23, 31, 34, 39
Cosmic, 22
Cosmopolitan, 51
    Religion, 51
Couch, 31–36, 39, 48–49, 53, 62
    Reclining, 33–36, 48, 53, 61-62
Cretan, 52, 55–56
    Feast, 52
Crete, 23, 40, 71
Crucifix, 59
Cruciform, 27, 29, 49–51, 54–59
    Figure, 27, 29, 49–51, 56-59
    Graffiti, 59
    Herms, 50, 55–56
    Sides, 55
    Structure, 55
Crypt, 53
Cult, 8, 14–15, 23, 27, 30–33, 39–41, 43, 46, 49, 51–52, 54, 57, 61–62, 64, 69, 71
    Association, 54
    Building, 26
    Group, 31, 53
    Municipal, 62
    Mystery, 39, 51, 58, 65
    Nature, 17, 26
    Place, 43
    Public, 52, 54
    Triadic, 62
Cycle, 12, 52
    Life-death-revival, 52
    Of Dionysos, 12
    Resurrection, 52
Cylindrical, 36, 61, 63
    Basket, 63

Dancing, 30, 39
    Ritual, 39
Daniel Cilia, 20, 63–64
Delos, 17–18
Delphi, 51, 53
Demeter, 23, 34, 39, 51, 62, 70
    Temple of, 23
Differentiation, 19
    Social, 19
Dining, 19, 33–35, 53
Diodorus Siculus, 52, 67
Dionysiac, 12–13, 15, 31–33, 35, 39, 51–54, 58–59, 64, 71
    Activities, 58
    Celebrations, 58
    Cowherds, 31-32, 35
    Cult, 33, 53, 59
    Festival, 15, 39
    Festivities, 13
    Imagery, 12
    Mystery, 12, 39, 58, 64
    Myth, 51

Procession, 15
　Ritual, 12
　Scenes, 54
　Theme, 52
Dionysian, 32, 34, 51-53, 55, 57
　Association, 34
　Cult, 51
　Festivals, 53
　Iconography, 57
　Motifs, 32
　Mysteries, 52
　Religion, 51, 53
Dionysos, 8, 12–15, 31–34, 39, 51–58, 60, 62, 65, 70
　Botrys, 12, 34
　Cretan, 55-56
　Crucified, 58
　Cult, 8, 14–15, 33, 51, 62
　Mask, 12–14, 34, 56-57
　Mysteries, 53-54
　Myth, 52, 55
　Old, 53
　Oriental, 55
　Sacrifice, 51
　Worship, 8
　Zagreos, 51–52, 54–55, 58, 60
Divine, 11, 13–14, 19–22, 26–27, 34, 41, 43, 56, 58, 60, 70
　Beings, 60
　Christ, 58
　Presence, 21–22, 26–27
Doliche, 60
Domestication, 18, 71
Domme, 59
Dordogne, 59
Dorian, 41
　Houses, 41
Drama, 2, 12
　Performances, 2, 12
Durability, 61
Dura-Europos, 16
Dushara, 53
Dwejra, 1, 6, 9–10, 46, 57
　Bay, 6, 9
　Inlet, 6, 10
　Valley, 6

Economy, 62
Edward Perry Warren, 13
Egypt, 52, 68-69
Egyptian, 14–15, 51–52
　Culture, 51
　Gods, 15
　Merchants, 15
　Myth, 52
Eleusinian, 51
　Mystery, 51
Eleusis, 39, 62
Enclosure, 24, 26, 40–41, 43–44
　Wall, 24, 26, 40–41, 43–44
Enculturation, 18
Engagement, 18–19
　Bodily, 19
　Sensual, 19
　Spiritual, 19
Enigmatic, 49, 70

Entablature, 27
　Horizontal, 27
Epigraphist, 47
Epithet, 51, 55
Eretria, 23
Erotes, 56
　Winged, 56
Eschatological, 51
　Ideas, 51
Escol, 58
Etruscan, 57, 70
　Style, 57
Europe, 40, 72
Evolution, 50–51, 71
Excavation, 2, 26, 66
Excavators, 23, 26–27, 30–31, 35, 37, 43, 48, 61, 66
Expeditions, 21, 67
　Nautical, 21
Extraction, 6, 8, 23, 31, 40
　Stone, 6, 8, 23, 31, 40

Farm, 7
　Complex, 7
Fatima, 14
　Fatima's Hand, 14
Fazzān region, 39
Ferruccio Barreca, 23
Figural, 13, 26, 41–43, 46, 50–51, 56, 60, 62
Flavius Josephus, 41, 67
Folk, 53
　Tradition, 53
Fontana, 6
Forecourt, 29
Fossa, 58
　Type, 58
France, 59, 68
Funerary, 42, 45–46, 63–65, 68, 71
　Context, 42, 45, 63
　Features, 42
　Monument, 63–65
　Nature, 63
　Repertoire, 63
　Sphere, 45
Fungus Rock, 9

Geographical, 6, 41, 51, 62, 72
　Boundaries, 41, 51
　Location, 62
Geological, 18
　Surroundings, 18
Ġgantija, 1, 4, 41–42
Għajn Abdul, 6-7
Għajn il-Kbira, 6
Għajn Tuta, 6
Għarb, 1, 6–8
Għar Dalam phase, 6
Għar Gerduf, 7
Għar Ilma, 6
Gift, 13
　Votive, 13
Globigerina, 6, 23
　Limestone, 6
　Stone block, 23
Gozo Archaeology Museum, 8, 11, 27, 43, 66

Gozo Museum of Archaeology, 7–8, 11–12, 39–40, 43, 48
Graeco-Roman, 53, 70–71
    Art, 53
    World, 53, 71
Graffiti, 57, 59
    Mediaeval, 59
    Votive, 57
Grapes, 8, 11-12, 58
    Pressing, 8
Greece, 31, 34, 40–41, 45, 51, 53, 62, 67, 70–71
    Ancient, 41, 45, 53, 62
    Central, 51, 53
Greek, 4, 12, 15, 26, 31, 41, 45, 51, 53–54, 62, 68–72
    Mysteries, 51
    Region, 31
    Terracotta mask, 12
    Tradition, 26
    World, 15, 51, 53
Guardia, 16
Guardian, 13, 20–21, 40
    Deity, 13, 20–21
Gudja, 59
Gymnasium, 41, 45

Hanno, 21
Haràm, 26
Hekate, 41
Hekate Epipyrgidia, 41
Hellenistic, 51–55, 71
    Art, 55
    Influences, 54
    Times, 51, 54
Herakleia-Perinthos, 34
Herodotus, 52, 64, 67
Herm, 13, 41–42, 50, 55–56
Hermes, 41, 50
Hermitage, 60, 63–64
Hierarchical, 35, 61
    Arrangement, 35, 61
Hinterland, 3, 9, 20, 22
History, 2–3, 41, 51–52, 67–69, 72
    Maltese, 3, 68
Historical, 3, 69, 72
    Period, 3
Holy, 38, 40, 72
    Water, 38
Horn, 42
    Of Consecration, 42
Humanised, 50
Hybrid, 4, 58–59, 61
    Culture, 4
    Religion, 4

Iconic, 56, 62
Iconism, 50–51, 62
Identification, 13, 21, 43, 49
Identity, 5, 34, 59–60, 65, 68–70
    Common, 60
    Cultural, 5
    Maltese, 5
    Religious, 59, 65, 68
    Sense of, 34
Imitation, 12, 27, 50
Immortality, 52

Independence, 58
    Square, 58
Indulgence, 53
    Sexual, 53
Initiation, 19, 35, 38–39, 52–54, 58–59, 61, 65, 68
    Ceremony, 65
    Rites, 19, 38–39, 52–53, 58–59
    Rituals, 52, 61
    Throne, 54
Initiatory, 53, 61
    Shrine, 53, 61
Institute of Near Eastern Studies, 2
Integration, 18
Interpretation, 8, 49, 60
Isis, 52, 67
Isolotto di Su Cardolinu, 23, 25
Isthmus, 31
    Of Corinth, 31
Italian, 2, 16, 70, 73
Italy, 1, 17, 51, 54, 62, 69–70
    Late Roman, 54
It-Tokk, 58
Ivy, 8, 12
    Leaves, 8, 12
Ix-Xaqqufija, 7

Janus, 41
Jean Hoüel, 63, 65
John, 3, 41, 67
Jonah, 13, 67
Jordan, 29, 53
Joseph Bezzina, 7
Joseph Calleja, 34, 47, 49, 58
Journal, 2, 68–72
    Papers, 2
Julia Domna, 7

Kabeiroi, 53
Klinai, 31, 53
Knights Hospitallers of St John, 3
Kommos, 23, 72
Kore, 34, 39, 62

Landform, 18, 72
Landmark, 18, 20–21
    Natural, 18
Landscape, 2–3, 18–19, 23, 68–73
    Physical, 2–3, 18
    Religious, 2, 18, 68
Law of the 12 Tables, 63
Legacy, 3, 68
    Material, 3
Lemnos, 53
Levantine, 43
    Tradition, 43
Liber, 62
Libera, 62
Libya, 1, 39
Life, 2, 19, 23, 51–52, 57, 61, 63, 70
    Daily, 2
    Maritime, 2
Ligortino, 40
Liminal, 17, 19–23, 60
    Character, 22

Place, 60
Sanctuary, 23
Space, 17, 21
Zones, 19-20, 23
Lipari islands, 3
Lithograph, 63, 65
Litholatry, 43
Littoral, 20
Locus, 26
Lot casting, 11
Lucius Septimius Severus, 7
Lunar, 40, 46
Lykosoura, 39

Macrobius, 12, 51, 67
Magna Graecia, 62
Magna Mater, 52
Management, 18-19
Spiritual, 19
Manes, 63
Marginality, 62
Maria Giulia Amadasi Guzzo, 47-48
Maritime, 2, 8-9, 11, 14, 19-20, 23, 46, 57, 61, 68, 70-71
Associations, 20
Community, 57, 61
Connections, 9, 19, 61
Environment, 19
Life, 2
Sanctuaries, 11
Maryland, 55
Mask, 12-14, 34
Materiality, 61, 70, 72
Mdina, 1, 3, 63
Mediaeval, 7, 27, 59-60
Date, 27, 59
Period, 7
Times, 60
Mediterranean, 1-4, 15, 17, 19, 40, 46, 51-52, 58, 62, 68-69, 72
Central, 4, 68-69, 72
Context, 2-3, 46, 68, 72
Eastern, 51, 58, 68
Island, 1, 3
Region, 3
Societies, 62
Western, 4, 15, 51-52, 58
Megalithic, 6-7
Remains, 6
Structure, 6-7
Megalopolis, 41
Megara, 41, 45
Melikertes, 31
Melite, 3, 63, 68
Menhir, 42
Mensae sacrae, 39
Menzel Harb, 26, 69
Messene, 41
Michelangelo Cagiano de Azevedo, 2
Military, 3-4
Exploitation, 3
Mineral, 6
Resources, 6
Minoan, 42, 55-56, 69
Gem, 55-56
Missione Archeologica Italiana a Malta, 2-3, 66-67

Mithraea, 32, 35, 60
Cave-mithraea, 60
Mithraic, 60
Reliefs, 60
Mitreo delle pareti dipinte, 35
Modern, 4, 6-7, 13-14, 31-32, 50, 70-71
Period, 7
Monasticism, 59
Rural, 59
Monumentalisation, 18
Monumentality, 22
Morality, 57
Moscow, 12
Mount Parnassos, 51, 53
Mtarfa hill, 64
Municipalia Sacra, 62
Municipia, 62
Murder, 66
Museo Nazionale Romano Palazzo Massimo, Rome, 50
Museum of Fine Arts, Boston, 12-13
Muslim, 4, 13
Mutilation, 27
Mycenae, 40
Mysia, 31
Mystery, 12, 39, 51-54, 58, 61, 64-65, 68, 71
Celebrations, 53, 58, 61
Collective, 54
Cults, 39, 51, 58, 65, 68
Dionysiac, 12, 39, 58, 64, 71
Bacchic, 12, 58, 64
Groups, 53, 71
Hellenised, 52
Of Dionysos, 51-54, 58, 65
Pagan, 58
Sanctuary, 53
Myth, 51-52, 54-55, 57, 65
Deity-related, 65
Mythographer, 51

Nabataean, 45
Nephesh, 45
National Archives Gozo, 10, 33
Nautical, 21, 46, 68
Symbols, 46
Navigation, 9, 21, 46
Necropolis, 45-46, 68
Neolithic, 3-4, 6, 69, 72
People, 3
Times, 6
Networks, 3, 11
Commercial, 3
Maritime, 11
Trade, 11
New York, 55
Metropolitan Museum of Art in New York, 55
Niche, 27-29, 31-33, 36, 56-59
Cultic, 31-32
Nicola Attard Montalto, 8
Nile, 14, 52
Nocturnal, 32
Rites, 32
Nora, 45, 50
Normans, 3
North Africa, 9, 72

North-African, 58
Notabile, 63–64

Occupation, 3–8, 63, 66
    Human, 6-8
Ochre, 8
    Red, 8
Offering, 12, 24, 26, 28, 30, 35–37, 39–41, 43–44, 47–49, 58, 61
    Table, 24, 26, 28, 30, 35-37, 39, 41, 43–44, 47–49, 61
Oinochoe, 8
Orient, 45
Oriental, 51, 55, 69
    Cults, 51
    Religions, 51
Orientalising, 51, 53
    Period, 51, 53
Orpheus, 51
Orphic, 51, 54
    Initiations, 51
    Myth, 54
Orphism, 51, 69
Osiris, 52, 67
Ostrogoths, 4
Oxford, 55–56, 68–73

Palaeo-Christian, 58
    Catacombs, 58
Palaimon, 31
Palmyrene, 16
Pannonia, 54
Pantelleria, 3
Pantheon, 11, 20
Patina, 23, 30
Pausanias, 41, 45, 67
Pavement, 27, 30, 35–36, 48, 61
Pedestal, 43
People, 2, 6–9, 11, 15, 18–20, 23, 58–59, 62, 71
    Maritime, 2
Perception, 18, 60, 70, 72
Perennial, 6
    Spring, 6
Performance, 19, 39, 51, 60, 62
Pergamon, 31–33, 35, 39
Peripheral, 4, 17, 62
    Location, 17, 62
Persephone, 51–52, 62, 64
Petra, 29, 53, 73
Phenomenon, 22, 42, 49–50, 58, 65, 69
Phoenician, 4, 7, 16, 18, 21, 46–47, 51, 54, 68
    Deities, 51, 54
    Domination, 4
Phrygian, 53
Pickaxe, 27
    Marks, 27
Piety, 57
Pillar, 40, 45, 69
    Betylic, 40
Pine, 52
    Tree, 52
Pivot, 23
Place, 7, 11, 14, 16–18, 22–23, 37, 39–40, 43, 45, 47, 51–53, 59–63, 66
    High, 17–18, 20, 22
    Prominent, 11, 16, 18

Plains, 3
    Fertile, 3
Plaster, 23, 25–27, 30–31, 35, 43
    Creamy white, 43
    Fine, 25, 30
    Fragments of, 23, 25–27, 30, 35
Platform, 26, 30, 36, 41
    Altar-like, 26
    Rock-cut, 30, 41
Plinth, 46–47
Plutarch, 52, 67
Podium, 31–32
    Temple, 31
Political, 3–4, 11
    Control, 3
Pool, 1, 19, 30, 36–40, 59, 61
Portal, 40
    Shrines, 40
Poseidon, 21, 31
Prehistoric, 3, 6–7, 26, 40–42, 45, 68–69, 71–72
    Burial, 6, 42
    Contexts, 45
    Megalithic structure, 7
    Period, 6
    Phases, 7
    Temples, 26, 40-42
    Times, 6, 42
Prehistory, 3, 72
    Maltese, 3
Preliminary, 2, 66, 73
    Report, 2, 66, 73
Presence, 3, 6–9, 13, 16, 20–22, 26–27, 32–33, 36, 41–42, 46, 57, 64
    Divine, 21–22, 26–27, 57
Priests, 15, 41, 52
    Itinerant, 15
    Lay, 52
Procession, 30, 39, 55
    Marriage, 55
Products, 7, 14, 40, 62
    Agricultural, 7
Promontory, 6, 9, 16–18, 20–23, 26, 45–46, 61
    Coastal, 6, 45–46
    Rocky, 26
Prophet, 13
Proserpina, 62, 64
Protector, 13, 20
Psalm, 41
Publicia Glycera, 63
Publicia Irene, 63
Pula, 50
Punic, 2, 4, 15, 23, 25–27, 30, 33, 36–37, 45, 50, 54, 60, 62, 68
    Counterpart, 15, 33, 62
    Funerary inscription, 45
    Mortar, 30
    Period, 2
    Pottery, 27
    Tradition, 27
Purification, 19, 37, 39
    Rites, 19, 39
Pushkin State Museum of Fine Arts, 12
Pyxis, 54
    Ivory, 54

Quadrangular, 1, 17, 23, 26–27, 30, 43, 46, 61
    Plan, 23
    Room, 27
    Structure, 17, 23, 26, 43, 46, 61
Quarry, 58

Rabat, 1, 3, 58, 63
Rabato, 63–64
Ramp, 17, 39
Ras ir-Raħeb, 1, 20–23
    Promontory, 20–23
Re-birth, 52, 63
Reconnaissance, 2
    Exercise, 2
Reef, 10–11
Refuge, 19
Relationship, 5, 18–19, 22, 60
    Enduring, 18–19
    Material, 18–19
    Spiritual, 19
    Symbolic, 18–19
Religion, 4–5, 14, 18, 51, 53, 62, 68–72
    Ancient, 51
Religious, 2–3, 5, 11, 18–20, 23, 27, 37, 39–42, 44, 51, 53–54, 58–60, 63, 65, 68–69, 71–72
    Activity, 40
    Assemblies, 53
    Associations, 53-54, 71
    Behaviour, 60
    Belief, 40, 42
    Character, 2
    Context, 2–3, 27, 37, 39, 42, 44, 63
    Groups, 54, 58-59
    Ideas, 59
    Identity, 5, 34, 59, 65, 68
    Influence, 51
    Pluralism, 59
    Scenario, 2
    Sites, 2
    Sphere, 3, 5
Repertoire, 2, 27, 63
    Ceramic, 2, 27
Reports, 2–3, 9, 66–68, 73
    Museum Annual Reports, 3, 67
    Preliminary reports, 2, 66, 73
Representation, 8, 11, 13, 27, 34, 36, 43, 45, 49, 52, 56-57, 63
    Three-dimensional, 57
Resonance, 18
Resources, 6, 19, 61
    Marine resources, 19
    Mineral resources, 6
Restoration, 25–26, 30–31, 35
    Programme, 31
Resurrection, 52, 58
Revival, 52, 58
Rhyton, 42
Rites, 19, 32, 38–39, 51–53, 58–60
    Initiation, 19, 38–39, 52–53, 58–59
    Of Passage, 39
    Purification, 19, 39
    Secret, 51
Rock-cut, 1, 8–9, 17, 27–36, 38–39, 41, 48–49, 53, 61, 70
    Cave, 17, 28-31, 53
    Features, 1, 17, 61

    Structures, 17
Roman, 2, 4, 7, 26–27, 30–32, 35, 40, 43, 51–55, 58, 60, 62–65, 67–72
    Authorities, 62
    Control, 4
    Date, 26, 31, 35
    East, 43
    Elements, 4
    Emperor, 7
    Forms, 27
    Funerary monument, 63–65, 68
    Imperial period, 62
    Occupation, 4, 63
    Period, 2, 30, 32, 35, 51–53, 58, 62
    Pottery, 27
    Sarcophagus, 52, 55
    Times, 7, 27, 51, 58, 65
    World, 4, 53, 68, 71–72
Rome, 2, 4, 17, 50, 52, 55–56, 62, 69–71
Route, 9
    Sea-route, 9
Russia, 63–64
Rustic, 26
    Technique, 26

Sabatino Moscati, 45, 50
Sabazios, 53
Sacral, 11, 20, 40, 52, 71
    Points, 11, 20
Sacrality, 40, 42
Sacred, 13, 18, 20, 23, 26–27, 36, 38, 40–43, 47, 49, 53, 57, 60, 65, 68–72
    Character, 20, 27, 36, 40-42, 47
    Meal, 57
    Precinct, 27, 36, 40, 47, 49
    Space, 60, 70-71
    Stones, 40, 43
    Structures, 26
    Trees, 40
Sacrifice, 13, 42, 51–52, 71
Sanctity, 40–41
San Dimitri Point, 1, 9
San Lawrenz, 1, 6–8
Santa Luċija, 1, 6
Santa Marija, 59
Sant' Antioco, 36–37, 50
Sarcophagus, 52, 55
    Roman, 52, 55
Sardegna, 1, 23, 25, 36–37, 45–46, 50, 71
Scallop shell, 63
Scenario, 2, 15, 42, 59
    Cultural, 2
    Religious, 2
Schematic, 27, 49–51, 56
    Figures, 27, 49–51, 56
    Symbol, 49
Screening, 28–30, 34–35
    Wall, 28–30, 34–35
Seascape, 19, 21–22
Seasonality, 52
Sea-wave, 8
    Decoration, 8
    Pattern, 8
Sect, 53

General Index

Secret, 53
Semi-anthropomorphic, 49, 51, 60
   Figure, 49, 51
Semi-figural, 13, 41–43, 50–51, 56, 60, 62
   Form, 50–51
Semi-iconic, 56
Semitic, 21, 53
   World, 53
Settlement, 3, 6
Shadrapa, 15, 33–34, 54, 62
Shelter, 9–10
   Temporary shelter, 9–10
Ship, 12–15, 23
   Cars, 15
Shipwreck, 12, 16, 21, 71–72
Shrine, 13, 21, 42, 47, 53, 56–58, 60–61, 63
   Aedicular, 63
Sicilian-Arabs, 3
Sicily, 1, 3, 6, 9, 51, 62, 72
Sicyon, 45
Signal station, 16
Significance, 3, 7, 9–10, 14, 18–19, 22–23, 28, 30, 35, 40–43, 46, 57, 59
   Religious, 19, 23, 41
Silenus, 55
Skorba, 1, 4, 41
Sloping, 17, 19, 35
   Profile, 17
   Promontory, 17
Social, 11, 18–19, 34, 60, 69, 72
   Groups, 18, 34, 60
   Power, 60
Society, 5, 18, 22, 72
   Maltese, 5
Solar, 46
Sources, 3, 21, 67
   Freshwater, 21
   Primary, 3
Spatial, 27, 35, 71–72
   Marker, 27
Spiral, 35, 47–48
   Rendering, 35, 48
Spirits, 22, 40, 42, 45
   Powers, 22
Spiritual, 18–19
   Forces, 18–19
   Power, 18
Springs, 6–7
   Għajn Tuta Spring, 6
   Perennial, 6
Stamnos, 13
Steatite, 40
Stela, 14, 27, 46, 50
   Sacrificial, 14, 46
Stern, 13–14, 46
Steve Attard, 11
Stone, 6, 8, 13, 17, 23, 26–27, 31, 35–36, 39–43, 45, 47–49, 72
   Extraction, 6, 8, 23, 31, 40
   Quarrying, 8
   Worship, 43, 47, 49
St Petersburg, 63–64
Stratigraphy, 2
Subsistence, 6, 23
Subterranean, 56

God, 56
Sulcis, 50
Supernatural, 22, 40, 42
Symbolism, 19, 63, 73
Symposia, 52, 58
Syncretism, 59
Syrian, 17, 51
   Deities, 51

Ta' Dbieġi, 6
   Hill, 6
Ta' Kerċem, 1, 6–7
Tal-Lunzjata, 6
   Valley, 6
Tanit, 14, 23, 45–46, 49
Tar-Rokon, 7
Tarshish, 13
Tarxien Phase, 6, 42, 72
Ta' Sannat, 58
Tas-Silġ, 1, 4, 36, 40, 42, 46–47, 61-62
   Sanctuary, 4, 36, 40, 42, 46–47
Ta' Xaqqufiet, 7
Telesterion, 61
Temenos, 24, 26–27, 30, 40–41, 43–44, 61
   Threshold, 26, 30, 40–41
   Wall, 24, 26-27, 40–41, 43-44, 61
Templar, 59
   Knights, 59
Temple B, 23
Temple period, 3, 6
   People, 3
Tenedos, 51
Termination, 27, 40, 47–49
Thanksgiving, 11, 16, 23
Tharros, 45–46
Theatre, 31
Thebes, 53
Thorikos, 31
Thrace, 34
Thracian, 51
   Women, 51
Threshold, 23, 26, 30, 35, 40–42
   Arrangement, 26
Thucydides, 41, 67
Tiered, 39
   Arrangement, 39
Tinnit, 14
Tony Mercieca, 7
Tophet, 36–37, 50
Topographical, 3, 18
   Surroundings, 18
Topography, 6, 60, 68–69, 72
Toponym, 7, 16
Tor Marancia, 55–56
Totem, 13
   Animal, 13
Tour of Domme, 59
Trade, 8, 11, 14–15, 62, 68
   Seaborne, 15, 62
Tradition, 14, 26–27, 41, 51, 53
Transitional, 50–51, 62
   Stage, 50–51, 62
Travel, 19
   Safe, 19

Sea, 19
Treatment, 36, 41, 43–44, 48
   Surface, 36, 48
Triclinium, 29, 32-33, 35, 52, 54, 73
Triq il-Wileġ, 8
Triumph, 55
   Of Dionysos, 55
Tropaion, 13
Trophy, 13
Trough, 39
Troy, 51
Tunisia, 1, 26
Turkey, 31–32
Tympanum, 27, 63

Underworld, 51–53, 55–57, 64
   Deity, 51-52, 55-56, 64
University, 2
   Of Rome, 2
Urban, 5, 17, 45, 53
Urbanisation, 3
   Centrally-located, 3
USA, 55

Valley, 3, 6, 58
   Winding, 3, 6
Vandals, 4
Vatican Museum, 55–56
Verticality, 27
Vessels, 8–11, 13–14, 16-17, 21, 35, 42
   Sea-vessels, 9-10, 13-14
Victim, 52, 66
Victoria, 1, 3, 58, 66, 71
Villa Giulia Painter, 13
Vine, 14
Virgil, 12, 67
Visibility, 10, 20–21, 68
Viticulture, 8, 14
Votive, 12–13, 39–40, 57, 70
   Graffiti, 57
   Offering, 12, 39
   Purposes, 13
Vow, 16
Voyage, 11, 21, 70
   Safe, 11
   Sea, 21

Walters Art Museum, Baltimore, Maryland, 55
Wash-house, 6
Water, 1, 6–7, 21, 29, 37–38
   Supplies, 21
Wied Pisklu, 6, 8
   Pisklu valley, 6
Wilderness, 18
Wine, 8, 12, 14, 53, 62, 72
   Cargo, 12, 14
   Consumption, 8
   Container, 8
   God, 8, 12, 53
   Jug, 8
   Merchant, 12
   Press, 8
   Production, 8
Workshops, 40

Sanctuary, 40

Xagħra, 1, 42, 71–72
   Brochtorff Circle, 1, 42, 71–72
Xlendi, 1, 6, 9–12, 15–16, 34, 46, 57, 67–68, 72
   Bay, 6, 9-12, 34, 68
   Harbour, 6, 9–11, 46, 57
   Valley, 6

Żebbuġ Phase, 42, 71
Zeus Meilichius, 45
Zion, 41